THE INDIAN NOVEL WITH A SOCIAL PURPOSE

Edited by
K. VENKATA REDDY
P. BAYAPA REDDY

ATLANTIC PUBLISHERS AND DISTRIBUTORS

Published by
ATLANTIC PUBLISHERS AND DISTRIBUTORS
B-2, Vishal Enclave, Opp. Rajouri Garden, New Delhi-27
Phones : 5413460, 5429987

Sales Office
4215/1, Ansari Road, Darya Ganj, New Delhi-02
Phones : 3273880, 3285873, 3280451
Fax : 91-11-3285873
e-mail : gupta.atlantc@axcess.net.in

ISBN 81-7156-855-6

Typeset at
APD Computer Graphics, Delhi

Printed in India at
Mehra Offset Press, Delhi

PREFACE

As a creative process, fiction is an expression of the most intimate awareness of the society in which it is born and in which it evolves. Small wonder, therefore, if the evolution of fiction and the evolution of consciousness of societal apparatus are simultaneous and interlocked. Indian English fiction which stuck deep roots in the Indian soil has had inextricable links with the socio-political milieu since its inception. By imaginatively treating the contemporary themes, the Indian English novelists sought to explore and interpret India significantly in its various aspects — social, political, economic and cultural. And, inspired by the vision of a just social order, they artistically expressed the urges and aspirations of people who were heroically involved in the struggle for equality and liberty. They have also been able to portray powerfully the real grandeur of the poor and the downtrodden and their ability to remake the world. Hence, the far-reaching significance of the Indian novel with a social purpose, and more so the need to assess it critically with a view to bringing out its salient features and highlighting its artistic achievement.

Though Indian English novel has received a good deal of critical attention over the years, the social purpose with which a large number of novels have been written, has eluded the serious concern of many a critic. The present book, consisting of twenty-nine papers contributed by scholars from different parts of the country, seeks to bring out the contours of the Indian novel with a social purpose though it can in no way claim to exhaust all its relevant aspects. It is divided into two parts, A and B. PART A deals with the Indian novels originally written in English and PART B with the Indian novels originally written in regional languages and translated into English.

PART A consists of nineteen articles. In his Introduction to the book K. Venkata Reddy makes an attempt to offer a brief account of the exigencies of socio-political history of the country that gave a momentum to the growth and development of Indian English Novel with a social purpose which is put in its proper perspective. Jaganmohana Chari seeks to provide a philosophical background to social purpose as motif in Indian novel in English. Naturally, Mulk Raj Anand, with his humane concern for the underdog, attracts the most critical attention. In his own article, "The Sources of Protest in My Novels" Anand makes a fervent plea for the need for the novel with a social purpose. Sarat Babu's paper points out how Anand's first novel, *Untouchable*, lays bare the hardships and humiliations the depressed and the oppressed suffer in a deformed Indian society. Rajappan examines *Untouchable* in the light of Marxist and Gandhian ideologies with a view to showing the novelist's envisioning of a new social order. T.V. Reddy brings out succinctly the class conflict between the workers and the owners of the tea plantations in Anand's *Two Leaves and a Bud* while Suneetha Rani in her paper treats the novel as dark drama of exploitation.

The only paper on R.K. Narayan by Mohan Ramanan explores fundamentally the question of Hindu civilization. While Rama Devi analyses Nayantara Sahgal's *Storm in Chandigarh* pointing out the problem of identity crisis at the individual, political and societal levels. Dr. Narendra explores the problem of violence in the three patriarchal institutions — the family, the society and the state. M.S. Nagarajan shows how the East and the West meet in Salman Rushdie's short fiction, *East & West*. Prema Kumari Marshal discusses *Midnight's Children* as a novel about Indian independence, the partition and its aftermath.

In their papers on Rama Sarma's *Look Homeward*, Meera Bai and Ashoka Rani deal with the problem of brain-drain and also of individual's responsibility and commitment to one's own country respectively. Somanath's paper on the rural novels of Romen Basu exhibits markedly the steady progression from non-violence as the means of social reform to full scale violence as the means of establishing a large-scale economic order.

Shashi Deshpande's works have also received some critical attention. Raghupathi discusses the self-assertion of the protagonist in *Roots and Shadows* while Lakshmi Narasaiah in his paper on *That Long Silence* points out the most determined social assumptions of Shashi Deshpande. Bayapa Reddy's paper on T.V. Reddy's *The Vultures* shows how the recent novel recreates the rural life enmeshed in traditional ills. P. Ramamoorthy's paper is on Gita Metha's *A River Sutra* that celebrates life and life-affirming impulses struggling against Death and life-negating forces.

PART B comprises ten articles which deal with the Indian novels written with a view to rousing social consciousness. Chellappan's scholarly paper on Chinappa Bharati's powerful novel, *Sangam*, presents its portrayal of the life of the exploited is close to Levy Strauss's structuralist analysis of the lives of the primitive tribes. Marudanayagam's article on *Verukku Nir* explores the Gandhian-myth. Gopala Krishnan Nair discusses the conflict between feudalism and humanism on the one hand, and secularism *versus* progress on the other, in *Thakazhi's Scavenger's Son* and *Two Measures of Rice*. Murali Ganam's paper is on Ramakrishnan's powerful novel *Verukkal* which seeks to exhibit the conflict between conservatism and progress faced by an orthodox community. Vijaya Guttal's analysis of Shivaram Karanth's *Choma's Drum* explores the social problems of the poor and the downtrodden, and also of the deprivation and exploitation in the large context of the human predicament. Visweswara Rao ably examines Malathi Chendur's preoccupation with the ideological impulsions of the freedom struggle in her novel, *Hridaya Netri*. Sree Devi's paper on Uppala Lakshmana Rao's *Athadu-Aame* reveals that the novel is a fervent plea for the participation of women in politics. H.S. Brahmananda in his paper on Unnava Lakshmi Narayana's novel, *Malapalli*, shows how the author achieves a harmonious fusion of Gandhism and Russian socialism. In her paper on Mukul Kesavan's *Looking Through Glass* Babli Gupta pleads that the novel could be read more meaningfully as a creative text of subaltern history than as a mere historical novel. Krishna Sarma's paper on Kasthuri Srinivasan's *The Light from Heaven* projects the novel as an earnest attempt to present the problem of caste in South Indian society.

The editors express their deep sense of gratitude to all the contributors but for whose sincere effort and unstinted cooperation the present volume would not have been made possible. It is hoped that the book will be of considerable interest and use to both the teachers and students of Indian English fiction.

–EDITORS

CONTENTS

Preface iii

PART A

1. Introduction 1
—*K. Venkata Reddy*

2. Social Purpose as Motif in Indian Novel in English 9
—*A. Jaganmohana Chari*

3. The Sources of Protest in My Novels 18
—*Mulk Raj Anand*

4. Social Deformity in Anand's *Untouchable* 30
—*Manchi Sarat Babu*

5. Synthesis of Marxism and Gandhism in Anand's *Untouchable* 35
—*C. Rajappan*

6. A Crusade Against Social Exploitation : Mulk Raj Anand's *Two Leaves and A Bud* 45
—*T. Vasudeva Reddy*

7. A Dark Drama of Exploitation : An Approach to *Two Leaves and A Bud* 51
—*K. Suneetha Rani*

8. R.K. Narayan's World-View in *The World of Nagaraj* 61
—*Mohan Ramanan*

9. From Apathy to Liberation : A Study of Nayantara Sahgal's *Storm in Chandigarh* 69
—*N. Rama Devi*

10. Non-Violence, Freedom and Equality in *Storm in Chandigarh* 76
—M. Narendra

11. The East and the West Do Meet : An Approach to Rushdie's Short Fiction 85
—M.S. Nagarajan

12. History as Protest : Salman Rushdie's *Midnight's Children* 94
—Prema Kumari Marshal

13. The Problem of Brain Drain in M.V. Rama Sarma's *Look Homeward* 103
—K. Meera Bai

14. Commitment to The Motherland : Rama Sarma's *Look Homeward* 110
—T. Ashoka Rani

15. Sociological Values in Romen Basu's Rural Novels 118
—P. Somanath

16. Self-assertion of Woman : Shashi Deshpande's *Roots and Shadows* 125
—K.V. Raghupathi

17. Life Inside the Cage : Shashi Deshpande's *That Long Silence* 132
—G. Lakshmi Narasaiah

18. Rural Life Enmeshed in Traditional Ills : T.V. Reddy's *The Vultures* 138
—P. Bayapa Reddy

19. Triumph of Desire over Renunciation : Gita Mehta's *A River Sutra* 145
—P. Ramamoorthi

PART B

20. A Synthesis of Socialist and Structuralist Perspectives : Chinappa Bharati's *Sangam* 154
—K. Chellappan

21. A Gandhian Novel with a Difference : Rajam Krishnan's *Verukku Nir* 160
—P. Marudanayagam

22. Conflict between Feudalism and Humanism : Thakazhi's *Scavenger's Son* and *Two Measures of Rice* 168
—N. Gopalakrishnan Nair

23. Conservatism Versus Progress : Ramakrishnan's *Verukkal* 177
—M. Murali Ganam

24. A Dreadful Plight of an Untouchable : Shivaram Karanth's *Choma's Drum* 182
—Vijaya Guttal

25. Ideological Impulsions of the Freedom Struggle : Malathi Chendur's *Hridayanetri* 188
—C.R. Visweswara Rao

26. Plea for Participation of Women in Politics — Uppala Lakshmana Rao's *Athadu Aame* 194
—K. Sreedevi

27. Gandhism and Socialism in *Malapalli* 203
—H.S. Brahmananda

28. Guilt and Atonement — Mukul Kesavan's *Looking Through Glass* 211
—Babli Gupta

29. A Modern Pilgrim's Progress : Kasthuri Sreenivasan's *The Light from Heaven* 219
—S. Krishna Sarma

PART A

1

Introduction

K. VENKATA REDDY

> "I hold that a novel must have a social purpose. It must place before the reader something from the society's point of view. Art is not necessarily for art's sake. Purposeless art and literature which is much in vogue does not appear to me as a sound judgement."
>
> —*Bhabani Bhattacharya*

The Indian novel, we may say, has emerged not simply as a pure literary exercise, but as an artistic response to the socio-political situation existing in the country. For, the factors that shaped and moulded the growth of the Indian novel, since the mid-nineteenth century, arose as much from the political and social problems of a colonized country as from indigenous narrative traditions of ancient culture. This is exquisitely exemplified in the Bengali novels of Ramesh Chandra Dutt, Bankim Chandra Chatterji, and Rabindranath Tagore in which "the socio-political situation existing in the country is faithfully mirrored right from the early phase of reformist exuberance to the growth of a revolutionary consciousness among the common masses of India."[1] If R.C. Dutt brought realism and reform to the Indian novel (*Sansar*), if B.C. Chatterji invested the Indian novel with a feeling of patriotism and revolution (*Anandmath*), Tagore had breathed into the Indian novel social relevance and psychological depth (*Gora* and *The Wreck*).

The struggle for Independence in India was not merely a political one, but an all pervasive experience that became a part of the life of almost all the sensitive and enlightened Indians. Parallel to this struggle for political freedom was a social struggle — a fight against superstition, casteism, poverty, illiteracy, and many other social evils that were eating into the vitals of Indian society. The socio-political movement that had caught the imagination of the entire nation also inspired the Indian novelists in English who rightly realised that novel too had a vital role to play in it.

Small wonder, therefore, if the Indian novelists in English, right from the end of the 1920s, started turning away from the romantic phase focusing their attention on contemporary problems. Motivated by the political and social questions arising from the changed historical situation they began to conceive of the relationship of man and his surroundings in a new and realistic manner. Though they did not completely break away from the central concern of man's quest for self-realization, they modified it by no longer emphasizing only its spiritual nature. As Dieter Riemenschneider rightly puts it, "the question arising from the new direction in the Indo-English novel is, then, to ask how the writers responded to this challenge and what they achieved in their efforts to portray, creatively and in a realistic manner, the effects these changes had on India."[2]

On top of that, the formation of the All India Progressive Writers' Association in the 1930s made the creative writers portray the Indian peasantry and the toiling masses in the hope that social transformation could be feasible only through mobilising the opinion of the underprivileged classes — the economically exploited, the politically subjugated, and the socially oppressed Indian populace. Naturally, the Indian English novelist realised that his salvation lay not in reproducing the imitative voices of his colonial masters, but in "seeking the strength and fertility of his own cultural sensibility and socio-cultural experience."[3] This realization on the part of the Indian English novelists resulted in the creation of a socially purposeful literature remarkable for its intellectual maturity, technical sophistication and artistic vision — all fused into an organic whole.

The Second World War, communalism and the partition of the country were the other historical forces that gave an impetus and a momentum to the Indian novel with a social purpose. There was enough material in the society torn by political manoeuvrings, social disparities, communal frenzy and corruption in bureaucracy for the thematic treatment by the Indian novelist to stir the imagination of the people to a new awakening. This made the Indian English novelist realize that "so long as the imagination of people is not stirred, the seeds of reform will keep lying on the road to be trodden upon by the unwary traveller."[4]

Thus, inspired by the exigencies of socio-political history of the country, the Indian novelists took upon themselves the responsibility of giving artistic articulation to the problems that beset the common people and their joys and sorrows, the crusade against the tyranny of poverty, illiteracy, suffering, superstition, caste and sex. Resulting, in a number of novels the protagonist is a farmer, a labourer, a factory worker, a patient or a virtuous woman pitted against a zamindar, a landlord, a factory owner, or a ruthless, callous hard-hearted man. We may say that, on the whole, Indian English novelists have succeeded in their efforts to portray creatively in a realistic manner the rural as well as the urban India. They not only present the various problems — social, political, economic and cultural — of the contemporary society but also offer solutions in terms of fictional art. They also reflect the challenges posed by the influx of Western ideas and concepts of the individual, the family, society and the relationship of Indian culture to other cultures.

The status and predicament of women in Indian society has been yet another motivating force for the Indian novelist with a social purpose. Despite the fact that woman can contribute to social regeneration as much as to the cause of family welfare, she became a victim of social prejudices and male chauvinism. However, Gandhi's clarion call to the Indian women to participate actively in the freedom movement made them conscious of the much needed liberation and equality of opportunity in personal, social and political life. Recognizing the potential of women to join their counterparts in their struggle against ignorance, superstition and backwardness, Indian English novelists in general, and women novelists in particular, began to treat women as legitimate subjects for their purposeful social novels. Their endeavour was to be relevant to their culture by presenting characters and situations rooted in Indian ethos. This is made clear by what Nayantara Sahgal proclaims :

> To be relevant to his culture, a writer's imagination has to be able to create the men and women and situations of the Indian environment and the Indian reality. If a writer can do this, make people feel with him, stimulate thinking, and inspire action because of what he writes, then he is fulfilling his function.[5]

The Post-Independence Indian English women novelists like Kamala Markandaya, Anita Desai and Shashi Deshpande present women in their heroic struggle to break through the pattern of sexuality and sensuality and to discover themselves as human beings capable of playing a positive role in the development of society.

In its constant growth and development, the Indian novel written with a social purpose can be distinguished through two sub-groups. First, there are novels depicting the political, economic and social oppression of individuals with their authors taking a humanitarian stance. We can include in this group K.S. Venkataramani's *Kandan the Patriot* (1937), Mulk Raj Anand's works in general and his *Untouchable* (1935), *Coolie* (1936), *Two Leaves and a Bud* (1937), in particular, Raja Rao's *Kanthapura* (1938), Bhabani Bhattacharya's *So Many Hungers* (1947) and *Music for Mohini* (1952), Kamala Markandaya's *Nectar in a Sieve* (1954) and *A Handful of Rice* (1967), Nayantara Sahgal's *Storm in Chandigarh* (1969) and *A Situation in Delhi* (1977), Salman Rushdie's *Midnight's Children* (1981), Amitav Ghosh's *Circle of Reason* (1986), Upamanyu Chatterjee's *English August* (1988), Shashi Tharoor's *The Great Indian Novel* (1990), and Chaman Nahal's *The Salt of Life* (1991) to cite but a few instances. In the majority of these novels the rebellious protagonist is integrated into society. Novelists like Anand and Bhabani Bhattacharya, however, insist on man's capacity and self-determination to work out his destiny for himself, thereby overcoming his conflict with society.

The second group centres on an individual's search for identity as in Anand's Trilogy — *The Village* (1939), *Across the Black Waters* (1941), and *The Sword and the Sickle* (1942), B. Rajan's *The Dark Dancer* (1959) and *Too Long in the West* (1961), Bhattacharya's *He Who Rides a Tiger* (1954), Markandaya's *Some*

Inner Fury, Khushwant Singh's *I Shall Not Hear the Nightingale*, A. Hossain's *Sunlight on a Broken Column*, Ranga Rao's *Fowl Filcher* (1987), and Shashi Deshpande's *That Long Silence* (1989). In these novels an individual character is shown as either unable or unwilling to accept the social role that the traditional society imposes upon him or her. The dramatic conflict usually arises out of the contradictions between Western notions of the autonomy of the individual and Hindu or Muslim concepts of supra-individual society.

The Indian English novel with a social purpose can be said to have stuck deep roots in the Indian soil, by imaginatively treating the contemporary problems and artistically exploring and interpreting India in all its variegated aspects. All the same, some critics contend that the Indian novel with a social purpose neglects the fate of the individual in a particular human situation in that it does not deal with a personal and private predicament. But, what we have to keep in mind is that, dealing as they do with a social milieu, these novels are more concerned with presenting the entire picture of society than with the individual's personal history. Moreover, we have to realize that in the works of a genuine artist there is no conflict between the individual and the social. The dialectics of their interrelation, as propounded by Hegel, is so strong that "the more the individuality of the artist stands out, the more actively he expresses the mood of his contemporaries — in short, the more partisan his approach. For those who are not disturbed by paradoxes, one might say that the more individual the artist, the less he belongs to himself, for the more individual he is, the more people need him."[6]

Critics may also argue that since the Indian English novel with a social purpose is mainly concerned with the contemporary problems and topical events in life, it may cease to have a universal appeal. But it must be remembered that the Indian novelist with a social purpose, like any good creative writer, writes with a social consciousness born of the phenomenon enacted around him. He is essentially a creative artist and realist who moves around the society and experiences the crises and tensions of the struggling classes, thereby arousing his deep creative impulse. We have to realize with Hippolyte-Adolphe Taine that a literary work is "a transcript of contemporary manners" and, from such "monuments of literature" we might recover "a knowledge of the manner in which men thought and felt."[7] It is also to be noted that "contemporary novels are the mirror of an age, but a very special kind of mirror, a mirror that reflects not merely the external features of the age, but also its inner face, its nervous system, coursing of its blood and the unconscious promptings and conflicts which sway it."[8]

A serious charge generally levelled against the novels written with a social purpose is that of tendentiousness and didacticism. Some of the committed novelists like Mulk Raj Anand and Bhabani Bhattacharya have been even accused to indulging in social and political propaganda. No doubt, the novelists who write consciously with a sense of commitment have their messages, to implicitly convey in the depiction of socio-political conditions, while relating the inner consciousness of mind and feelings of heart to the outer landscape of the social milieu. All creative artists reveal some truth, and more so the novelists who are in direct involvement with socio-political situations. This is exquisitely driven home to us when Joan Rockwell, in her seminal work, *Fact in Fiction : The Use of Literature in the Systematic Study of Society*, points out :

> Fiction is not only a representation of social reality, but also a necessary functional part of social control, and also, paradoxically, an important element in social change. It plays a large part in the conduct of politics and, in general, gives symbols and modes of life,... in those less easily defined, but basic areas such as norms, values, and personal and interpersonal behaviour.[9]

It is, therefore, not right to argue that the main task of an artist is with his craft rather than with social reform inasmuch as it smacks of didacticism. What we have to bear in mind here is that the creative artist unlike the philosopher, the sociologist or the journalist does it not in "cold statements of dogma," but only in terms of life rendered artistically through various fictional devices and techniques. Therefore, as Asnani observes, "the novelist has no reason to fear the intrusion of didactic values lest it should contaminate the pure spirit of his creative endeavour."[10] What the novelist has to fear is not the didactic or ethical values themselves, but the wrong modes of their projection. This is laid bare when Bhabani Bhattacharya, a novelist of affirmation of life, asserts :

> Art must teach, but unobstrusively, by its vivid interpretation of life. Art must preach, but only by virtue of its being a vehicle of truth. If that is propaganda there is no need to eschew the word.[11]

So, novel, as an art form, can certainly seek to convey a message 'unobstrusively' in so far it is 'a vivid interpretation of life' and 'a vehicle of truth.'

Recent novelists like Romen Basu and Chaman Nahal go a step further and maintain that unless fiction concerns itself with social reality and possesses specific humanism, it cannot be considered a significant work of art. Romen Basu observes :

> Fiction is a human document. For me, unless it has some bearing on real life it cannot be taken as a work of creation.[12]

Chaman Nahal is of the firm view that a novel must possess 'synchronic relevance,' and it must concern itself with "a specific community," a specific class, a specific society." He says :

> The main point is that an artist should be able to associate himself with an identifiable community, or what Raymond Williams has called 'a knowable community.'[13]

Above all, if the novelist is convinced that he is primarily an artist, and achieves a harmonious fusion of his social concerns and artistic norms by raising the themes above the didactic content, he will have no need to bother about the critics who label him a propagandist. Resenting the charge of overt didacticism and propaganda levelled against him, Mulk Raj Anand, a spokesman of the downtrodden and a lyricist of their joys and sorrows, feels sorry for his adverse critics who are not alive to the artistic presentation of his socially purposeful novels. He says :

> My adverse critics have seldom seen the symbolism, the attitudes and the rugged poetry beneath the prose. Therefore, if the attempt to discover the meaning of life in my human environment is propaganda, then I am a propagandist, otherwise, it is expressionism, which I define as an enactment of the body-soul drama of human beings, through the imagination.[14]

From this it is clear that in the best of the works of committed novelists like Mulk Raj Anand, Bhabani Bhattacharya and Kamala

Markandaya, the social purpose and the artistic excellence are fused together. Thus, it is not the social message, but the artistic presentation that carries the novel, and makes the social purpose vivid and poignant.

NOTES

1. Shyam M. Asnani, *Critical Responses to Indian English Fiction*, Delhi : Mittal Publications, 1985, p. 1.
2. Dieter Riemenschneider, "The Indo-English Novel," *Commonwealth Fiction*, edited by R.K. Dhawan, New Delhi : Classical Publishing Company, 1988, p. 50.
3. Shyam M. Asnani, *Critical Responses to Indian English Fiction*, p. 4.
4. *Ibid.*, p. 8.
5. Nayantara Sahgal, "The Indian Writer and the English Language," *The Statesman*, 9 May 1971 (Sunday edition), p. v : 5.
6. N. Shamota, *On Artistic Purpose*, Moscow : Progress Publishers, 1960, p. 107.
7. Hippo-Adolphe Taine, "From the Introduction to the History of English Literature" in *Twentieth Century Criticism — The Major Statements*, eds., William J. Handy and Max Westbrook, New Delhi : Light and Life Publishers, 1976, p. 309.
8. Walter Allen, *Reading a Novel*, pp. 18-19.
9. Joan Rockwell, *Fact in Fiction : The Use of Literature in the Systematic Study of Society*, London : Routledge & Kegan Paul, 1974, p. 4.
10. Shyam M. Asnani, "Towards a Closer Understanding of the Indo-English Novel," *Journal of South Asian Literature*, Vol. XVI, Summer, Fall, 1981, Number 2, p. 154.
11. Bhabani Bhattacharya, "Literature and Social Reality," *The Aryanpath*, Vol. XXVI, No. 9 (September, 1955), p. 394.
12. Romen Basu's letter dated May 19, 1992.
13. Chaman Nahal, *The New Literatures in English*, New Delhi : Allied Publishers, 1985, p. 110.
14. Mulk Raj Anand, "In Reply to M.K. Naik's Questionnaire," in M.K. Naik, *Mulk Raj Anand*, New Delhi : Arnold Heinemann, p. 176.

2

Social Purpose as Motif in Indian Novel in English

A. JAGANMOHANA CHARI

'Change' and 'social change', whether in life or literature, have ontological implications and ideological messages to convey. As far as 'change' in Indian Fiction in English is concerned, Adil Jussawala bemoans :

> ... And 'change' was the cry we rallied around at Independence. Change was what we thought would come over us when we overthrow the British norms, language and literature... But they have proved tougher than we thought, some of us have become *the new colonials* (emphasis added), and our expectation of ourselves has been false.[1]

The reasons for the failure of the Indian English writer seem to lie deeper in our culture and its clash with the British. Pittu Laungani identifies the factors contributing to the clash as :

Individualism	—	Communalism
Cognitivism	—	Emotionalism
Free-will	—	Determinism
Materialism	—	Spiritualism [2]

The broad categories of factors on the British side (on the left) derive from positivist-materialist-rationalist discourse; whereas the Indian (on the right side) could be termed, for lack of a better paradigm, traditional or spiritual or brahmanical discourse. And as Laungani observes, "Each of the above factors needs to be understood as extending along a continuum, starting at, say, individualism at one end and extending into communalism at the other,"[3] and *vice-versa*. So is the case with observations I am going to make in this paper about the British or the Indian, as a philosophical background of the problem on hand.

The rationalistic paradigm is hegemonic in that it believes in the control of nature and the world. It confuses freedom with power which was a bane of imperialism. It flows from the positivistic-agnostic-individualistic faith in the self and its experience through senses and to the exclusion of the other. The liberal humanist mind which is the product of rationalism when confronted with India which defied 'reason and form' and so was a muddle, was so baffled that the substitution of 'force' for 'civility' became a matter of natural transition for the coloniser. This is the theoretical tale of the British imperialism in India, according to E.M. Forster Vide *A Passage to India*.[4]

Reducing the problematic of *A Passage to India* which is an Anglo-Indian novel to an abstract theoretical construct is here called for because the novel poses some very important questions regarding 'social change' as well as Indianness. Coming to grips with the question 'what is India' is not easy unless you approach it with great clarity afforded not by intellectualism alone but with the emotional category of love or at least sympathy, as E.M. Forster did.

Forster, with his liberal humanist belief in personal relations as the crux of the rationalist world view with the parameters of individuality, unity of the universe and freedom including the freedom of man to commit religiously has undertaken to study India in the novel. He posits his three characters on the gamut of liberal humanist thinking : Mrs. Moore with her love of god or faith in Christianity, Adela Quested with her insistence on her own senses as a guide to experience and a painful awareness of the fallibility of the same, and Fielding whose intense faith in the world of men with a combination of "goodwill plus culture and intelligence," (p. 56) and a strong unwavering commitment to human values ("I'd far rather leave a thought behind me than a child," p. 110). The polyphonic search of these Forster's characters seems to have failed in different degrees in identifying the Indian reality and coming to terms with it, not on account of lack of sympathy, but because of the constraints embedded in their discourse.

The rationalist discourse of the West is structured by logical thought flowing from personal experience or senses. Self occupies a central place in it. Self and the objective world are pitted against each other. Therefore, the subject-object relationship tends to be mutually exclusive unless there is an active common interest present in it. This leads to gross individualism. To make the individuals stick together always, events or movements mostly political and violent in nature are required. Any personal pain or suffering on account of its individualistic nature acquires the character of violence without being relieved by the pleasure of sharing.

Adela Quested on account of this ontological essence in her personality finds the facts in India painful. Her future husband who used to subscribe to her world view before he came to India has now become a hard boiled imperialist like the other Britishers, Turtons and Burtons — intolerant, distrustful and disrespectful to the natives. The theory is : everyone who came to India would become a hard boiled imperialist in a year's time. Love of freedom and respect for individuality would turn out to be a love and respect for power. The invisible line between freedom and power gets worn out with the contradiction between the British self and the native reality which comes to the fore. It is exactly this contradiction which rose from beneath in her consciousness when Adela Quested in the company of Dr. Aziz began to think of the impossibility of her marriage to Ronny Heaslop "on that eternal rock" (p. 144) of the Marabar Hills. And that leads to the disaster everyone who has read the novel knows.

Even Mrs. Moore without a protective covering of the rationalist thought for herself and with intuitive sharing of emotions like an Oriental becomes a victim of the irrational primal reality of India, which she could recognise only as "something snub-nosed, incapable of generosity — the undying worm itself" (p. 198), the ontological being of India, not at all superior to the animal without a sense of evil or good. "Most of the inhabitants of India do not mind how India is governed. Nor are the lower animals of England concerned about England, but in the tropics the indifference is more prominent, the inarticulate world is closer at hand and readier to resume control as soon as men are tired," (p. 105).

It all boils down to one premise or postulate, typically Western or liberal humanist, that whatever is beyond the positivist metaphysic or discourse is considered non-human. It is this postulate which could explain what constitutes 'humanism' of the West. Its parameters of freedom, equality, brotherhood and the related concepts of individualism, development, enlightenment, and modernity are all part of the same discourse which is essentially hegemonic.

But, is the Indian ontological essence the same as characterised by the liberal humanist discourse — a mystery or muddle? E.M. Forster with his objective dexterity which is also part of the same discourse seeks to portray the Indian reality without allowing himself to be overtaken by a sense of racial incompatibility which had been rampant in the British circles.

Forster's description of the caves, the court room, the procession instantaneously organised after the court-verdict, and the religious procession at Mau celebrating the birth of Krishna and the echoes they produce is more or less a faithful version of the Indian reality as he understood. The different echoes — boum, esmis esmoor, or the susurration of rain, river, singing of the devotees and the peel of thunder without lightning, all put together are an expression of the essentialist response of the Indian consciousness or "spirit," not a "frieze" (p. 41). For the racially conscious Adela, it may look like a 'frieze' or the polished inside of a cave — mysterious but apparently innocuous. But if scratched it will give out a *boum* which could "undermine the hold on life" (p. 140) of the tresspasser.

The various activities or responses of life in India in which the masses are involved have all been fashioned and evolved by layers and layers of civilization from the depths of prehistory or the "Ancient Night" (p. 68). They make themselves felt as 'echoes' the modes of expression of collective 'existence' of its people.

No trace of violence could be seen in such massive responses or demonstrations because its spirit is not structured by logical thought flowing from individualistic experience or senses alone. The sense of devotion expressed in a religious response in India is not like Christianity in which there is the conception of the 'son of God' coming into being. The God himself is inconceivable to

Indian tradition. It is structured by the concept of *brahma*, the creator who exists in each human individual in transcendence of senses, logical thought and good and evil. It in fact pervades the whole universe. This response defies all Western imagination which could think of 'son of God' for itself and 'idolatry' for the adversary. There is no streak of violence in it, because there is no self involved in it; no trace of fear since devotionally it is an expression of the divine being in one's own self and no fury or fanaticism of faith as in religious campaigns of the Western hemisphere. This collective response is manifest as an expression of joy in the maker's love : 'God is love.'

It has no political design. On the contrary, the behaviour of the Indian community, as Forster seems to find has been so structured as to convert the force or energy in it into an acceptance of all forms of oppression like poverty, exploitation and inequalities by reference to God. Metaphysical in nature, this response has traditionally not been allowed to degenerate into violence.

To put it in a nutshell, the subject - object dichotomy does not exist in the case of an Indian untouched by the Western categories of thought or discourse. This very point seems to have been alluded to in Adil Jussawala's reportage of a story recounted by U.R. Anantha Murthy as told by a painter who attended an Indian Writers' Seminar :

> A painter who was then told a story which impressed Anantha Murthy deeply. He said that during his wanderings through villages in the North, he came across a hut in which he saw a stone. It was decorated with red powder and flowers which meant it was an object of worship. He asked the owner of the hut — a peasant — if the stone could be brought outside the hut since he wanted to photograph it. The stone was brought outside and the photograph taken. The painter than realized that he might have polluted the stone by shifting its position, and apologized to the peasant. The peasant said it didn't matter. He'd fetch another stone and anoint it with the powder. So, the painter said, *any piece of stone on which the peasant put the power became God for him. The objective and subjective were one in such a person* [emphasis added]. He belonged to the illiterate Indian mass — seventy per cent of the population. Western education had alienated

> those at the seminar from him and those like him. If they didn't understand the structure and mode of his thinking, they couldn't become true Indian Writers.[5]

The painter's argument allegedly disturbed Anantha Murthy, but he was already too bedevilled by the West to take the instance of "the authentic Indian peasant" but as "an imported cult figure of Western radicals reacting against their materialistic civilization."[6] Yes, the terminology ("authentic") is Western, true; but why think in the jargonese of the West and miss the point.

But, in my view, it is none of the mistakes of our present day writers. The process of mimicking started in the very days of colonial/imperialist connection. As we find it in the novel of E.M. Forster, there is Prof. Godbole, the erudite and orthodox Deccani Brahmin wearing a pince nez and wrist watch while dancing and singing ecstatically in praise of the God, Krishna, on the day of the Festival of *Gokulashtami* in the state of Mau where he serves as the Minister of Education. There is Dr. Aziz cherishing the memory of his deceased and beautiful wife with the help of a photograph and sharing the pleasure with a Britisher, Fielding in the novel.

Pince nez, wrist-watch and photograph as consumer items (they must have been imported items at the time) were the product of Western materialism and by the same count, taboo for the Indian orthodoxy and Moslem pardah. (Incidentally, A.K. Ramanujan says in one of his poems his orthodox Hindu grandfather was reluctant to being photographed for fear of losing caste).

Possibly, E.M. Forster was only able to observe those physical details of Westernization of Indian intelligentsia. The deeper and more subtle modes of mimicking of the West like in thinking and attitudinizing on the part of the upper strata of the Indian society he seems to have missed. But he knew for certain that real India was present not in them — the Bhattacharyas, Dases, Godboles, Azizes and on. It lived in people who are represented by "the man who pulled the punkah" (p. 207), the naked figure who sat on a raised platform near the back of the court room like "a male Fate, a winnower of souls" (p. 207). The god-like aloofness in him is unaware of the minute encounter between the East and West being acted out before his eyes. Forster finds a similar Indian soul in the crowds which followed the Krishna procession at Mau, the singers "sounding every note but terror" (p. 304) and in the 'servitor' who carried the village of Gokul in clay presided over by the silver image of Krishna on a tray and pushed it into the dark waters of the river as the monsoon rains raged as a rite which symbolises the unity of God with the human as well as non-human universe.

Even today, the illiterate masses of India retain the sense of unity with nature and the world around them creating no rupture in their consciousness. The same joy in sharing their pains and pleasures with others and the same silent suffering of inequities and exploitation and without a trace of violence in it could be seen in them. If any violence has crept into their midst it is only as a corollary of 'development' which has inundated the Indian scene as part of the Western discourse; and which is not only 'skewed' in favour of the rich and privileged but divisive also. But I am not concerned in this paper with the development of India or Indian masses, but with social purpose or change as motif in Indian fiction in English.

The Indian society which is largely traditional is governed by the categories of brahmanical discourse which constitutes, first the belief in Vedic and Upanishadic idea of all-pervasive *brahman* multiplied and diversified into so many cults; and second, *Varnashrama dharma*. The present day caste system is nothing but a minutely retailed reproduction of the original *Varnashrama dharma*. Like any other discourse it is universalizing but at the same time on account of the *Varna* (caste system), it privileges the few on upper levels creating the elite. This discourse has been a primitive remainder in the Indian society from the remote past and zealously guarded and preserved through successive foreign invasions, especially by the elite.

In their encounter with the colonizing imperialist who posed a far greater threat to their privileged position, the Indian elite could not withdraw and remain a "frieze," or act like a "spirit," to borrow Forster's tropes. Both passivity and resistance were suicidal for them because they had strong material interests to protect. The propertyless lower castes never were a threat on account of the spiritual thrust of their discourse. So they, *i.e.*, the elite were obviously in favour of meeting the British half-way on the line and reincarnate into a class which could bargain with the colonizer in their own language for a common end. In this respect, the hegemonistic character of both the discourses — the British and brahmanical made a smooth sail possible.

The British, on the contrary, felt threatened not by the elite but the god-like naked figures — the mass of India who rose like an echo or a wave which the British could not understand. They knew ways for controlling or subduing a member of the elite like Dr. Aziz or Godbole (or his maharajas) with their legal or political tentacles. But they knew no way to put down the echo or a procession of massive proportions.

But the Indian elite could count on the support of the poor naked wretches divided on caste-lines in their bargain with the British. Non-cooperation, salt-satyagraha, burning of foreign goods and *ahimsa* were used by this class to enlist the support of the masses to trounce the imperialist.

To make the long story short, the literature produced by this elite class both before Independence and after is fraught with a curious mixture of rationalist and brahmanical discourses. *Samskara* of U.R. Anantha Murthy is a case in point. Pranesha Charya in this novel goes on an individualistic quest for the non-dualistic (advaita) unity of castes and cultures; which is to say he sheds his caste with Chandri and savours it leisurely in aloneness.

Not many protagonists in the novels produced by them are picked from lower castes. Mulk Raj Anand's *Untouchable* and *Coolie*, Bhabhani Bhattacharya's *So Many Hungers*! and *He Who Rides a Tiger* are mere exceptions. They seem to have been written in the first flush of idealism afforded by Independence.

Afterwards Indian novel in English has taken strange forms — partition novel, existential novel, psychological novel, novel of expatriate experience, novel of magical realism, novel of mythical parallels and so on and so forth. But no novel which depicts community experience or struggles is to be found in Indian Writing in English except for Kolimantikunnadi (The Forge has caught Fire) by Allam Rajaiah. Only a few novels originally written in indigenous languages like *Godan* by Premchand and *Chemmeen* by Thakazhi Sivasankara Pillai are free from this bias.

Whatever social purpose which could be seen in Indian Fiction in English appears to be cosmetic and super-structural that too, pertaining to the life of the elite. The elite gradually began to encompass in its fold the successful middle class. And the protagonist more often than not constituted a composite figure constructed from the class of 'national liberators' like Gandhi, Nehru, Vivekananda and Annie Besant. Rabindranath Tagore's much praised *Gora* serves as an example here.

If there is any novel in the whole corpus of Indian writing in English and English translation in which the elite class and the rural mass are portrayed as real Indians without the cosmetic touch of either Western or Indian idealism it is, I think, Premchand's *Godan*, and Tagore's *Gora*.

NOTES

1. Adil Jussawala, "Being There : Aspects of An Indian Crisis," *The Bombay Review*, No. 1, 1989, pp. 20-27.
2. Pittu Laungani, "Cultural Influences on Learning : Contrasting Indian and English Experiences," *New Quest*, July-August 1993 (100), pp. 203-211.
3. *Ibid.*
4. The edition of *A Passage to India* consulted here is the Abinger Edition of E.M. Forster edited by Oliver Stallybrass and published by Edward Arnold, 1978. Quotations from this text are indicated by page numbers in parenthesis.
5. Adil Jussawala, *op. cit.*
6. Adil Jussawala, *op. cit.*

3

The Sources of Protest in My Novels

MULK RAJ ANAND

I

Various Studies of my novels by scholars have, in recent years, confirmed what I tried to show in the autobiography of my ideas, *Apology for Heroism*, as also in the confessional novels, that there has always been an emergent connection between my life and my writings, throughout my creative career. Of course, some critics have interpreted my obsession with truthful presentation of the realities of life as ideological realism. Quite a few members of our academic intelligentsia are addicted to terms of European critical theories which define "classicism," "romanticism," "realism," and "naturalism." These often make for abstract analysis of novels. They ignore the pressures of human life, the compulsions on the writer's conscience, which may be occasioned by miscellaneous inspirations. In the novel, one evolves characters and traces their motivations from the reservoir of the collective unconscious and individual diversities. Since the anarchy of feelings is indistinct, emotions are woven into the texture of fictional narrative from uncontrolled impulses what I call in the Punjabi phrase *Ghaon Maoon* which may mean *angst.*

Each novel might, therefore, compel internalist interpretation standards, not from principles of criticism, built on the western traditions. The novel arose in the 18th century, downwards, in backgrounds different from ours. Should our own fiction be judged as part of the western tradition? Our interpreters may have to sense the deeper layers of inner faculty and experiences of our own people, from the inherited oral cultures of our people in decay or renewal. In this way, the critics may be able to judge our fictional works, more creatively as they would then go to the sources of our insights in concrete human situations rather than through abstract theories that don't yield novels.

There have been pioneering critiques in the West of this kind from the study of sources of creations of novelists and poets, like those by Edmund Wilson in *The Wound and the Bow*, by D.H. Lawrence in his *Studies* in *Classic American Literature*, by John Middleton Murry in his *Son of Woman*, by George Lukas in his essay on Thomas Mann, and by Edward Thompson in *Rabindranath Tagore*. These examples have been lost on our commentators. Our critics unconsciously belong to the category described by Jean-Paul Sartre as being always in unhappy relationships with their wives who have to wait for them to come to dinner, because they can't tear themselves away from certain preconceived categories of responses to define each mood, feeling and idea.

Most of the critics who have written about my novels have not noticed that my fictions arose from the compulsions of life of the lower depths, where the rejected in our country have been condemned to live. I have reenacted their tragı-comedies again and again. The critics often treat my fictional works according to dates of publications, in chronological order, in the dominant Leeds University manner, where text is all. If the text reveals men and women in dirty clothes, soiled hands and perspiring faces, they are unsavoury. Said Edward Garnett : "We English don't like characters in rags to come into our drawing rooms!" And the Brown Sahibs feel the same way about novels which deal, as E.M. Forster once said, "with the seedy side of life."

II

I made my first conscious protest as a writer when I came away from Bloomsbury after hearing the critic Edward Sackville West declare : "There can be no tragic novel about the poor! They can only be laughed at, as in Dickens : The canine can't go into literature."

I was just then writing *Untouchable*. I left London and went to Gandhi's Sabarmati Ashram in 1927. There I learnt some sincerity, truthfulness and simplicity. The Mahatma sent me to the people before I should write any more novels. From that time onwards my protest about the human predicament, under the Empire, and in the atmosphere of our own decay, often resulting from blind acceptance of bad habits and the taboos of the sage Manu and the Hadith traditions of Islam, became self-conscious.

I persistently examined my own conscience. I had intimate experience of villages, small town people, big town grandees, and of life's little ironies, tragedies and struggles. All experience, then, became the reservoir from which I wrote my fictions, hoping to transform the raw material of life freely into communicable forms, rather than accept the mould of the objective form of Flaubert or Henry James' preciousness. Personal-impersonal as my novels are, based on my various experiences, and vicarious indulgences as a "pseudo poetic prose wallah" (someone once dubbed me), they are written by an "I" at some distance from myself and the characters. The resulting fictions may have sometimes seemed amorphous. Much as the novelist may try to control people's lives, the imperceptible feelings of characters, and their emotions and actions, tend to overflow, as in Balzac, Tolstoy and Proust.

My novels were intended to be different from those of others, departures away from the upper and middle section fictions. I wished to recreate the folk, whom I knew intimately, from the lower depths, the lumpens and the suppressed, oppressed, repressed, those who had seldom appeared in our literatures, except in Sarat Chatterji, Prem Chand, Bibhuti, Tarashankar and Maneck Bannerji.

I had realised after my stay in Sabarmati Ashram that I could not stand alone, always looking at the heavens where the gods live, because they were now hidden behind the twilight. I would face humans, especially the hollow-cheeked men with dazed eyes, the women who grew old, before they were young, from drudgery, forced childbearing and beatings from husbands, naked children, with distended bellies and big eyes, beggars whining for alms, my widowed aunts, my drunkard uncles, stalwart sepoys, Pathan frontiermen frightened of the Ferungis but carrying guns in defiance — in fact, men and women in a world reduced to slavery. "Daridranerayan" or the poor man-God incarnate, as Gandhi called the rejected, were the flesh and blood for me to worship. In the struggle for emergence, of which they were a part, each contact brought the sense of a certain sacredness. A new kind of religion was then emerging in my novels, a religion of love for people, which has been called Mulk's humanism. But having left philosophical system, I did not want to belong to any "ism" — even humanism. Worship of each character became a passion behind the writing. I accepted all the strengths and weaknesses of the people. Maybe empathy for human beings makes for a tenuous relationship enabling the novelist to remain within himself, and yet be with others, a pervasive relationship of leviathanic complexities. But characters are concrete human beings and not generalized symbols.

As the relationship between the author and others revealed the horrors of the inequalities, through which those above have perpetrated cruelties on those below generation after generation either through caste discrimination or the power of the Rajas over the Ryots or priests with their rigid ritualistic injunctions, I allied myself with the urges of men to free themselves through whispers of discontent or sighs in half-sleep or in violent and non-violent actions. In this way, I sensed the pain of life, which the more privileged took out of the weaker members of the flock. I knew the patriarchs who enslaved women by imposing conventions which curtailed their movement and made them always bow their heads until they became hunchbacked at forty behind the prison of purdah or semi-purdah. I was aware of the ignorance of the underprivileged who expiated their own miseries by lies and subterfuges, and the rich who were always in fear of losing their worldly wealth. I was aware of the Imperial state with its god and goddess, George Panjim and Mallika Mary, and later our own nouveau riche. As I gave up systems of philosophy and wrote from the human condition, I was unable to sleep easily. I woke up every morning to see how men and women dreaded other men and women, how they were always benthead before the White Sahibs and the Bania moneylenders, landlords and sarkari officers. There were millions of the disinherited who ate only one meal a day. If I could not physically "wipe every tear from every eye," as Gandhi said, we must do, I felt I could utter a thousand cries to wake up people from the weight of supine slumber. As every prayer of the folk was to an idol of a past dead myth, I felt I could create new myths of emergent man for myself and others who had become bundles of infantile disorders, suffering in the various seasons of hell under the reign of Yama, but like Narcissus looking at each other with cynical smiles. Only insights and outsights into the anarchic world might bring inner maturation to human beings. The terror of one's self may be got over by asking every day, as in the *Brihdaranyaka Upanishad* : "Who am I?" "Where do I come from?" "And where am I going?" I would have to recognise my own identity as an Indian, not subservient to the white rulers or the indigenous upstarts. I would have to be a man without the help of an anthropomorphic God. I knew it would be difficult to free men from all the fears, but I had hunches about freeing myself and some others, through my passion for breaking away from the accepted certainties and for rediscovering importances, the needs of men and women in travail.

III

As I felt many inchoate urges in the days of my growth, I came to awareness of things beyond the fixtures of *dastur* (custom) through daily experience of human misery and the pain of life. I saw the manḍalas of the gods of my mother, on which stood images of Guru Nanak, Krishna, Aga Khan, Yessuh Messiah and a snake engraved on the metal. I asked questions about them. They were not answered until my father, a fashionable Arya Samajist, told me that our ancestors had made thunder and lightning into Indra, the sky into Varuna, and the Sun into Surya. Gone was this exalted cosmic view in our time. But, in spite of explanations about the origin of gods, the God with a big beard, sitting on top of the sky, which most people believed in lingered in my fear-haunted imagination. So when a young cousin of mine died at the age of nine of tuberculosis, I wrote a letter of protest to God in heaven, asking Him how He could take away the little innocent girl who had committed no sin!

I noticed that among my playmates were boys and girls who were considered superior if they were the children of parents in big houses, and inferiors if they were the children of parents in small shabby hutments. Our parents asked us to have a bath after playing with untouchable children from the hutments, because we may have touched them. I early realised that since we were of the *Kshtriya* caste, we were "superior," with *Brahmins* above us, and *Vaishya* shopkeepers slightly inferior to us, and all outcasts far, far below us, forever branded from birth by *Varna ashram* the Hindu caste order! The cruelty of this God-ordained system came home to me when Bakha, a sweeper boy, brought me home bruised in the head by an accidental stone, and my mother scolded him for carrying me and touching me. She bathed me even though I was bleeding. This little incident was to remain in my conscious-unconscious, and became a passion for justice against the age-old fixtures of non-human discrimination against untouchables. This passion became the protest implicit in my first published novel, *Untouchable*. It was turned down by nineteen publishers before E.M. Forster wrote a preface. Since then it has been published in many languages of the world, and as a Penguin classic it has also been dramatised in London and Delhi and called a 'prototype of the protest novel in the newly freed world,' now emergent from dead habits, supposedly ordained by the supreme God. The opposition between the "superior" and the "inferior" had been obsessively in me long before I read Marx.

I became early aware of the anomalies of our family. My father belonged to the coppersmith brotherhood of Amritsar, who had worked for generations on the Golden Temple and made utensils. He went to a Christian School. On passing Matric, he joined the British-Indian army as a clerk. He observed the *dasturs* (customs) of the coppersmith brotherhood, even when he presided over the local Arya Samaj. On the other hand, as a "servant of the Sahibs" he had become a "Shadow Colonel" and adopted George V and God Almighty, *Anndaata*, giver of bread. Although read in advanced literature of the West, he agreed to arrange marriages with dowries for his two elder sons, which cut short their studies, and forced them to become a part of the order of Babus, used by the alien Sarkar for the routine work of the Empire.

The wedding ceremonies were performed in our house by Brahmins according to Vedic rites, burning good *ghee* to banish evil spirits. Prayers were pronounced in a language which not even the priest understood. Infinite repetition of high sounding words was necessary! The aim of the recitations was not to evoke thoughts but to perpetuate the supremacy of worship, *Pujapath*.

I once fainted as a boy when I saw a goat being butchered in a temple of Kali where my mother used to take me in our hometown. I never got over the revulsion from that murder. It is from my tenderness for living things that my indignation against the mumbo jumbo of barbarous rituals arose. I began to feel that living words of creative writing are inspired not by rhetorical repetitions but by maturing of insights, through experience of pain.

The incident which upset my own childlike admiration of the Pink Sahibs was insignificant enough. I saluted the Adjutant Sahib of my father's regiment and stared at him out of curiosity. He hit me with a cane and I went crying to my father who did not say anything but accepted the punishment I got for the crime of staring at the Sahib.

Later in April 1919, when Police Raj was declared by the alien Sarkar in Amritsar to stop the protests against the Rowlatt Act, forbidding gatherings of four people, I went out of our home to see what the curfew was about. I was caught by the police and kept chained to many others all night. Next morning I was given seven stripes of the cane by an Indian policeman under orders of the Anglo-Indian Superintendent of Police. I shrieked at the punishment. My mother came and rescued me, tearing her hair in the anger against the red-faced *afsar*. I could never forget her helpless rage against the police. When my father refused to notice the bruises on my body, I was confirmed in my dim feelings of rebellion against him and the Sarkar. I realised that the army and the police and the law were the Indian instruments of the King-Emperor, himself an instrument of the big Imperial machine that devoured human beings in the Empire.

I began to listen to the terrorists, who wanted to abolish those who made war on people by throwing bombs on the oppressors. Later, being too weak for such heroism, I listened to the message of non-violence of Gandhi. The Mahatma was talking of bloodless sacrifice, of accepting lathi blows against the staves and bullets of the ruling power. I felt the vast oppression from behind an invisible wall, which prevented the gods in Whitehall from listening to the Mahatma's "still small voice." In between there were the preachers of Christian ethics. But the rulers were stuffed-up dummies of an automatic power, hollow inside, while the abstract sarkar was an organized oppression, with bayonets and machine guns, which were to ensure the carrying out of the white man's burden of responsibility. Kipling's Indian native, "child and savage," accepted the hollow men as masters, so long as they got the paltry silver coins at the end of every month.

The primitivist expression, including the use of ugly words, epithets and staccato phrases, in my novels of the lost Utopia of childhood, shows that people had retained some sense of honour, as they felt that the rape of mother and sister was an insult. So the epithets used by them were not reproduced for sensational effect or stark realism but to create rough characters in all their authenticity.

So the alienation of my principal characters along with their hopeless ventures in freedom was presented in tragedies that are not "realistic" but expressionistic dramas of struggle between the poetic ambition of heroes to emerge from the depths of degradation and to recover their human inheritance. Only my new heroes-anti-heroes were not deliberately uplifted into a classical world, and presented in allegory. They were kept within the framework of human experience in a timebound world. They may become symbols of struggle and later appear as new mythical figures, representing youth urging towards freedom. But against the idea that their fate has been determined before their birth, they are only innocent humans struggling for the dawn in the darkness around them.

IV

My novels, then, are to me whirlpools where I have been able to see individuals in the chaos, in relative distinction from each other, and yet in the midst of indistinction. I have returned in each fiction to recognise some people in the undifferentiated mass. And in this recognition, from alliance, with them in pity, has been a kind of expiation of my burning conscience about the sufferings of men and women. The writing of each novel has been an effort to be with others, while remaining myself, in the area of freedom, which is love. If the life of each individual is in kinship with other lives and yet a unique mystery into which we can only have glimpses, every human being is a god or a goddess. Thus every insult, every humiliation, every deprivation, every lowering of dignity, must be protested. Because only by the love we give to others can we be human; only in the defense of the divine status of human beings have we the opportunity to end the alienation of men and women from themselves and from each other, brought by fear, petty differences, and the confusions of darkmindedness, which make them swarm around us as ghosts and demons of the night.

The yoke of pity has been carried by some of the most sensitive men in every generation in our land. It has relieved every age. As pity is, in essence, love, I have tried to rescue this love, which becomes love of life in every form, against hatred, which is the death of love. As the defiance of all those offences, injuries, deceits, lies and murders of the body-soul, becomes holy anger, my protests are an expression of my holy anger.

As love is the core of human relations, the very first need of men and women from which comes procreation, family, the social group, and the state, we have to see how, in the evolution of life, the old primitive tokens, totems and taboos have survived and been accepted as eternal inspirations in the name of tradition. So much so the cautionary words and images, which were to sanctify and preserve human relations as sacred, have been made abstract or perverted, and life has often been sacrificed in the name of religion. That is why the poet Iqbal cried out from the depths of our degradation in the early years of our century :

> To tell the truth Oh Brahmin old,
> The idols in they temple have grown cold.

Therefore, in my novels, which seek to recreate living human relations in all their intricacies, I have been compelled to be concrete ("realistic" as the critics like to put it). I have tried to look at the realities of life, hoping that each day might be a new day of happiness with a new sun, a new moon, with new people, who may inherit the good thoughts of the past, but may look to the future. This may have meant wandering through the labyrinths, but one can recognise one's own face and the faces of others not by grovelling before fixed images but by living experience of men and women through a religion based on tenderness.

My characters were not meant to be revised versions of old mythical symbols of the epics. I think that human beings do change in a changing universe, even if ever so little. So old mythical characters like Sita, or Savitri, or Rama , are not eternal types who must be repeated in new incarnations. We cannot live by the good and bad examples of gods and kings of five thousand years ago. My characters are thus conceived as human beings of a different historical age which is not the changeless *samsara* of tradition. They struggle in this life, on earth, in the here and the now, even if their struggles end in failures. Or they grope in the dark, and then emerge here and there, through our new contemplations, giving glimpses of the still mysterious universe defined in the past through fear but now being revealed through adventures in the heavens and on earth.

My new myths also aspire to some hypotheses of the "religion of man," though I do not subscribe to even this as religion. Every happenstance can lead to fresh realisation of space-time change on our earth, revolving around the sun in a precarious balance being upset by arrogant men. The writers and the artists are ever in search of new myths to escape fixations. Many old certainties dissolve. Some, which are relevant, are assimilated. But changes of style in art and literature are due to the crises of creativeness, when men and women in their search for freedom renounce the old dead symbols to create new myths, to grow and renew the jaded, habit-ridden personality. Renewal is eternal. Otherwise men remain dead-in-life. Renaissance is the cue for all human passions to grow, ever in freedom, to higher consciousness.

V

Apart from the essentiality of metaphorical protest about the human predicament in a time in which the gods have failed or become irrelevant, mine is the willed extroversion of hope against despair, if perchance the monolithic state should break down through its own mechanical failures. I feel that war is the ultimate sacrifice of victims, in which both the victor and the vanquished face death which is made the arbiter of human destiny by men of power. The dehumanisation of man reaches its apotheosis in the armed subjection of people. The cruelty and barbarism of absolute power, sanctified by the past Rajas of one kind or other, may not be acceptable to the erstwhile slaves. The sacrifice of human life cannot go on forever. I admit that few men have risen to become gods in our transitional age. Humanity in the mass faces the institutional violence of the modern omnipotent state, even when it professes participation of peoples in democracies. Every new Spartacus fails, because the state refuses to wither away. The old authoritarianism of the Egyptians, the Greeks, the Romans, the Chinese and the Indians comes back. The fascist slogan commands us like the ancient patriarchs, "to believe, to obey, and to fight." The new dictators put up enemy dummies and announce "Laser war" against their enemies. Bloody sacrifice of one mass against another is asked for by the new incarnations of Caesars! Still only war can confer on the barbarian conqueror the title of God! Never mind the cost in the possible nuclear war which may be the death of mankind!

The failure of the neo-idealists is that they are too refined to look at the gift horses in the mouth and to protest, because they rediscover themselves in a frozen art. They do not wish to include human cause (which includes political, social and psychopathic alienations) in "polite" fiction.

To be sure, creative arts reflect life in a mirror. But the concave mirror is also a mirror. And one does not always talk only with one's own face in the mirror. The mirror is other people. The love of Narcissus for himself makes him feel he is a god. Others are not admitted as his kin. He alone is himself, his Self, which means he has become God Almighty. Therefore, he is no more human.

The novels about human beings need the author, and others, men, women and children, in the whirlpool, where there are contrary impulses, clashing trends, doubts, misgivings, making life a river which flows, often caught in whirlpools, and then rushing in waves towards the ocean. Each human being as an individual brings his own repressed culture and to express himself through signs, broken speech and attitudes. His or her personal myth is born of facts and fantasies. In a novel there are elements which are indeterminate, particular and concrete. The contrary impulses reflect confusions. If the novelist liberates his characters, and they take charge of their own destinies, fiction may release their inner sentiments and feelings and action, dissolve the taboos of religion, or the state, and reveal their predicaments, which by themselves may lift the burden of pain and anxiety and make for transcendence which is ecstasy.

The reader often says, then, on reading a genuine novel : "Oh! I too feel like Dostoevsky's Idiot, or Tolstoy's Natasha, or Prem Chand's Hari."

The emptiness of ritualistic rhetoric has already given place to the sense of humanity in the significant novels of our age, through the exaltation of life against death. The humanist novel speaks in living speech, often in passionate frenzies, from the uprush of spirit, to express the predicament of men and women. The new novel thus exorcises the monsters and terrors of dissolution from the hell on earth, made by some for others. Sartre was right when he spoke figuratively that "Hell is other people." I would only revise the phrase by saying that "Hell is some other people!"

The novel is for the world's continuance. It is urged by the wish to express oneself in uneasy syntax, in dim perspectives and from vague feelings of those who seek to break the shackles of serfdom. It is inspired by the urges for many freedoms, baulked by the demons of power. It is against the insults, injuries, deceits, lies, hypocracies, the mortifications and murders, brought by men become monsters and for the celebrations of the simple pleasures of the miracle that is life in its span of "four score and ten," given to us by some accident of nature, which we have often exalted and frequently degraded!

The protest novel is the source of renewal of the human person.

●

4

Social Deformity in Anand's *Untouchable*

MANCHI SARAT BABU

Civilization, the Bhasmasura of mankind, has evolved through the interaction of three processes : division, hierarchization and privatization. In the first process, human beings have divided themselves into various fragments, depending on gender and labour. The second process had done the grading of those divisions while the third has brought about private family add private property. The social hierarchy, private family and private property formed a strong nexus. The nexus has evolved an exploitative and oppressive society where the minority, through the juggling of civilization, enjoys the wealth produced by the hard labour of the majority. Exploitation and oppression have deformed the human society greatly.

The social deformity has taken the form of caste system in the Hindu society. There are four recognized classes called 'Varnas' and one unrecognized class called 'avarnas'. They are Brahmins (priests, teachers and ministers), Kshatriyas (kings and warriors), Vyshyas (tradesmen), Shudras (craftsmen) and Panchamas (menial workers). Shudras and Panchamas are again divided into various castes and the castes are hierarchized. Ambedkar therefore aptly points out, 'Caste system is not merely a division of labourers — which is quite different from division of labour — it is an hierarchy in which the divisions of labourers prevents them from being united and makes them exploitable. Moreover Manu, the Hindu law-giver, says, 'A Brahmana may compel a Shudra, whether bought or unbought, to do servile work for he is created by the Creator to be the slave of a Brahmana' (p. 148). He prescribed draconian punishment to Shudras for reading the Vedas and for insulting higher caste people.

Panchamas whom even Shudras consider inferior have been ill-treated, oppressed and exploited more than Shudras for ages. They are considered untouchables and forced to live far away from caste Hindus.

Mulk Raj Anand's *Untouchable* depicts graphically the hardships and humiliations that Panchamas suffer. It exposes the ugly deformity of the Hindu society. The novelist does it just by narrating the life of Bakha, an untouchable boy during one day.

Bakha is a son of Lakha, the Jemadar of the sweepers of the town and cantonment. He is eighteen years old. He gets up early in the morning and goes to work at dawn. He cleans three rows of latrines several times single-handedly. Yet he remains comparatively clean. In spite of the reveries that he indulges in, he does his work efficiently and the hard toil makes him very strong. Anand says :

> Each muscle of his body, hard as rock when it came to play, seemed to shine forth like glass, 'What a dexterous workman!' the onlooker would have said. And though his job was dirty, he remained comparatively clean (p. 16).

Like a devoted doctor of the society, he prevents several infectious diseases from attacking the caste-Hindus by cleaning their latrines and sweeping their roads. Yet the people who enjoy his services never treat him with a little compassion. On the other hand, some of them humiliate and hurt him.

The Panchamas are forced to live away from the village. They cannot use the well in the village as Caste-Hindus think that their mere touch pollutes it. So the Panchama men and women have to wait at the well for a long time until a caste Hindu is kind enough to draw water from it and pour it into their pots. Sohini, Bakha's sister faces the same fate in the Novel. 'She balanced her pitcher on her head and went to and fro her one-roomed home to the steps of the caste-well where she counted on the chance of some gentleman taking pity on her and giving her the water she needed' (p. 24). She and others quarrel among themselves for the chance of getting water and abuse one another using 'inter-caste recriminations.' None of the caste Hindus who take water from the well feel kind enough to pour water into their pots.

After a long time, Kalinath, the priest who badly needs physical exercise as a remedy for his constipation agrees to get water from the well for the low caste people who assemble there for water. He draws a pail of water with great difficulty. He sees Sohini and feels enchanted by her youthful beauty. He therefore drives others away and pours the water into her pot. Then he orders her to come to his house to clean the courtyard. When she goes to his house, he seeks erotic pleasure from her. Feeling frightened, she screams loudly. He shouts at her and accuses her of polluting his holy home. A crowd of angry caste-Hindus gather there to scold Sohini. At the moment, Bakha arrives while sweeping the streets. He feels furious at the injury and insult but he controls himself. He sends his sister home and himself goes to collect food from the rich Hindus. Since he is not a girl, he is less successful than his sister in collecting food.

Bakha returns home after collecting food. He expresses his resentment of the ill-treatment by caste-Hindus. He bitterly says to his father 'They think we are mere dirt because we clean their dirt!' But his father does not react as he expects him to. He tells Bakha how he has been cured of a serious illness by Baghwan Das, a local doctor. He accepts the Hindu law of untouchability though he is not happy about it. This shows how each parent generation internalizes the social hierarchy which it transmits to the next generation psychoculturally. Thus Panchamas become their own enemies by taking for granted their inferiority and the superiority of caste-Hindus which are culturally programmed as rightly argued by Srilata Batliwala in her brilliant article, 'Why do women oppose women?' The oppressed people like Bakha resent and rebel against caste distinctions when they are young. But they yield as they grow old. This is because the psychocultural acceptance and observance of caste distinctions by almost all the people proves more powerful than the physical force that the high caste-Hindus may use in preserving them.

Bakha gets a pair of old breeches from Tommy and a pair of old boots from a soldier. He daydreams that he looks like a civilized white foreigner by wearing the breeches and boots in the 'fasshun!' In the afternoon he attends the marriage of his friends sister whose higher caste prevents him from marrying her. The love shared by him and his playmates in their friendship dissolves their caste distinctions for the time being. So he, Ram Charan a washerman's son and Chota a leather-worker's son eat sugar-plums together at the marriage. They plan to play hockey in the evening. Havildar Charat Singh treats Bakha affectionately and presents him a new hockey stick. Bakha forgets his caste and feels happy in his presence.

Bakha and his friends play hockey in the evening. He plays very well and makes a goal. The rival group feels jealous about it and this leads to a quarrel among the players. During the fight, a high-caste little boy falls down and hurts himself. Bakha takes pity on him and lifts him up. The boy's mother sees it and rushes to the spot. She angrily scolds Bakha for polluting her son. Feeling miserable and frustrated, Bakha returns home. But his father rebukes him for wasting the afternoon and drives him out of the house. Bakha's cup of sorrow is full and he leaves the house. This exemplifies the plight of the children of lower castes who are deprived of the joys of childhood that the children of higher castes enjoy.

Anand's novel does not end here. The remaining part of the novel is a kind of epilogue. Bakha feels greatly frustrated and looks for a way to end his agony. He meets Colonel Hutchinson, the salvationalist who offers him a solution for his problem. He is asked to get converted into a Christian to end his caste. Many low caste people have accepted Christianity to attain a respectful status in Indian Society. But Bakha does not choose this solution. Then he attends a meeting addressed by Mahatma Gandhi who says, 'I regard untouchability as the greatest blot on Hinduism'. Gandhiji calls the untouchables 'harijans' the people of God. He considers the idea of pollution Satanic. Bakha feels much encouraged yet disturbed by this. As he walks on, he encounters a third solution. The poet Iqbal Nath Sarbhar says that the untouchables can end their caste by changing their profession as the modern sanitary system will make this possible. Of all the three solutions, this impresses Bakha the most as Anand himself seems to favour it. Bakha finds great solace in it and feels relieved. Ambedkar also rejects the solutions offered by Christianity and Gandhism but embraces Buddhism to end caste distinctions.

It is sixty years since Anand wrote *Untouchables* and fifty years since we got Independence. But things have not changed any better and the social deformity of Hindu society has survived all the social reforms and revolutions. Badal Sircar in his play *Stale News* points out :

> Three — There were 3019 cases of atrocities on the Harijans in the first nine months of 1978. 175 Harijans were killed, 129 Harijan Women were raped, there were 289 cases of arson... (p. 134).

This happens every year. So K.R. Srinivasa Iyengar also comments in his concluding remarks on the novel. 'Almost 36 years after Anand's novel was written (1935) and 24 years after independence, the problem — with blunted edges, perhaps, and also with some relieving features here and there — still defies a firm and final solution! (p. 338). Girish Karnad in his play *Tale-Danda* shows how the high caste Hindus most inhumanly massacre the Sharanas of Basavanna only because they have performed a marriage between a Brahmin girl and a Harijan boy. Commenting on the contemporary relevance of the play, he remarks, 'It seems 800 years have solved no problems.'

We are back exactly where we started (p. 76). So it is evident that all the solutions — religious, social, political, legal and even technological — have utterly failed to cure the Indian Society of this ugly deformity. Perhaps it cannot be cured of until and unless the powerful nexus of the social hierarchy, private family and private property is destroyed totally. Until then, Anand's novel remains relevant.

REFERENCES

1. Mulk Raj Anand, *Untouchable*, New Delhi : Orient Paper backs, 1970.
2. K.R. Srinivasa Iyengar, *Indian Writing in English*, New Delhi : Sterling Publishers, 1984.
3. Dr. Babasaheb Ambedkar : *Writings and Speeches*, Bombay : Government of Maharashtra, 1987.
4. Srilata Batliwala, 'Why do women oppose women? *The Hindu*, Sunday Magazine, May 2, 1993, p. iii.
5. Badal Sircar, *Three plays*, Calcutta : Seagull books, 1985.
6. Girish Karnad, 'Where is the tradition? (Interview) *Frontline*, September 25, 1992, pp. 74-77.

5

Synthesis of Marxism and Gandhism in Anand's *Untouchable*

C. RAJAPPAN

India's economic impoverishment and the proletarianisation of the peasants as a result of colonial exploitation had left a deep impact on Anand. He became an ardent admirer of Hegel's philosophy. He acquired mastery in varied fields of Eastern and Western knowledge. Marx, a lover of humanity and a terrible opponent of social injustice stressed the role of economics in man's exploitation and enslavement. He sought mass involvement in socio-economic change. He raised the slogan of socialism. Mahatma Gandhi a great patriot, a humanist and a democrat fought for a better future for his people and all mankind. Marx and Gandhi were dissatisfied with the existing system and they felt the need for a transformation. The present socio-economic order causes frustration and Gandhi longs for a classless society. Man suffers from 'self-alienation'. Gandhi wanted to transform the state of 'self-alienation' into a state of 'self-realisation'. Marxism is based on economic foundation whereas Gandhism is based on moral structure. Gandhi and Marx were two outstanding personalities who influenced Anand profoundly.

It will be one of the aims of following discussion to point out the synthesis of Marxism and Gandhism in Anand's *Untouchable*. The crippling poverty, the paralysing slavery, the inhuman exploitation of the masses and the hypocrisy were the dominant forces that were crushing the Indian society. The complex problem that confronts Indian society is caste system. Actually in India there are four castes — Brahmana, Kshatriya, Vaisya and Shudra.

Though the caste system had a racial origin, it had also an economic element in that it represented a system of labour and of class-stratification. In the four fold vedic social order, the priest was the spiritual mentor and he was the leader of society. The priestly order became degenerated in course of time giving way to the birth of Kshatriyas. The kings too became selfish and ignored the interests of the humanity which paved the way to the establishment of the Vaishya rule. The Industrial revolution in England heralded the Vaishya rule. Later the Vaisya was alienated from society. It will be replaced by the Shudra, the proletarian.

Anand identified democracy with the rise of the Shudras which would bring mass awakening and progress. Marx gave his full hearted support to socialism. Anand was deeply moved by the misery of the vast masses in society. Marx's socialism was essentially materialistic in concept. Anand is for social ethics of non-exploitation and universal human welfare. Socialists and Communists are of the opinion that legislative reform or proletarian dictatorship will bring about a new society. According to Marx, the working class, was reduced as a result of capitalist exploitation. He wanted a total revolution. Anand recognised the role of working class in building a strong, united India. He was constantly aware of 'our national sin' of exploiting the proletariat for centuries together. They have been working silently without whining. They are forced into the depth that they cannot rise-try however they may. They sink lower and lower everyday. They have been pushed to the level of thinking that they are not human beings. According to Vivekananda :

> "the greatest national sin is the neglect of the masses and that is one of the causes of our downfall"
>
> (*Complete works of Vivekananda*, Vol. VII; p. 327-28)

Anand felt that the Karma theory unjustly justified all evils in Hindu society like untouchability, denying education, denying dignity of labour and denying even a modicum of social respect to certain castes.

Marx believed that religion was the opiate of mankind and that it must be done away in the interest of human welfare. According to Marx "religion is an illusion. It is unscientific and baseless. It is sought after to bring comfort to the afflicted and suffering." The advancement in scientific knowledge and technical skill has created an atmosphere that led to the ruin of man's affliction. Man is made to realise his potentiality. This is the essence of Marx's religion. In a class society, social oppression of the working masses and their apparent helplessness in the struggle against their exploiters gave birth to religion.

According to Anand love is the root of religion. Man cannot think about the attainment of happiness and immorality hereafter but he has to think about it here itself.

He can find real and absolute happiness in this very existence. Priests stood as middlemen between the worshipper and the worshipped. They created a gap between God and the worshipper which paved the way for opportunities for exploitation.

When Bakha the hero of the novel *Untouchable* reached the temple to see the Gods in the temple he was shocked to hear the words "polluted, polluted."

The priest said that he had been touched "I have been defiled by contact" (UT 68). 'But I... I...' shouted the lanky priest histrionically (UT 70). Anand silently comments on the attitude of the priest through the use of the word "histrionically." The concept of Bhakti has no meaning in day to day life. Bakha, an untouchable who is not even allowed to have a glimpse of the inner Deity joins his hands unconsciously and bends his head in the worship of the unknown God whereas instead of becoming one with God, the lanky priest thinks of seducing the untouchable girl Sohini even in the temple itself. The place of worship has been converted into a place of seduction by the so called priest. After doing all these things, he acts as if he were a holy person. Worship has lost its meaning. Sexual exploitation is a part of social exploitation. To satisfy his lust, Pandit Kalinath takes advantage of the lower social position of Sohini.

What Anand preached to the people was not weakening piety but life giving strength which is an embodiment of love. The aim of religion must be the welfare of humanity. In this aspect Anand and Marx come closer. According to Anand, religion is love, religion is understanding. Anand cannot be dubbed irreligious. What we want in our blood is pity, compassion and understanding.

As a humanist Anand deals with how man can be changed and how he can be relieved of the evils. The unnamed woman in *Untouchable* is religious. She is rich and she belongs to an upper class but she is kind and essentially humane.

She is not in contact with Western culture as Colonel Hutchinson is, but she remains essentially humane. Dignity of labour or equality which is known to Colonel Hutchinson is unknown to her. When Bakha is abused by the woman for having defiled her house by sitting on the doorsteps, the other woman treats Bakha kindly and calls him her son and advises him never to sit on people's doorsteps, "My child, you should not sit on people's doorsteps like this" (*UT* 81). She is the human being talking to the sweeper. Anand aims at the elevation of the downtrodden by preaching the brotherhood and equality of men and by pleading for a casteless society. He thinks that a fresh approach to human life is needed in this decadent society.

In the Interview *The Hindu*, December, 1983 to Anand has emphasised that in spite of his relentless attack on the evils of caste system the same evils continue. His analysis is still relevant. His main characters Bakha, Bikhu and Munoo are all protestors against the oppression under which these classes have been traditional sufferers. But the time in which they live was not ripe enough for constructive action. Intuitively Anand knew that more spontaneous protest on the part of the oppressed class will not lead to any solution to the thousands of year old evils in Indian society. Hence, his emphasis is on pity, sympathy and compassion on the part of the so called the upper classes. This is Anand's main achievement in his novels that he has induced in his readers these three emotions of pity, sympathy and compassion for the downtrodden in India. Anand, the saviour of the untouchable is of the opinion that the real salvation for the untouchables would come only when the people embrace compassion, pity and sympathy.

Marx, Gandhi and Anand were totally committed to the cause of the downtrodden. What touched Anand deeply was the miserable condition of the people, the slavery under which they were groaning, the oppression to which they were subjected for centuries. Marx was a fighter and so were Gandhi and Anand. Marx's philosophy was based on the concept of struggle for existence, class war and the concept of the survival of the fittest. Anand wanted the oppressed people to stand up united without fear. They should get educated and enlightened. Marx gave a revolutionary gospel to the poor and the downtrodden to change the course of history. He advocated hatred, organised violence and total destruction. His call is supposed to be an open call to violent revolution to destroy the existing social order and total destruction of all that he conceived as wrong and unjust.

Anand's aim is the same *viz.* the destruction of social order, but the means adopted by him to destroy the social order was Non-violence, a powerful weapon given by Gandhi. He does not believe in his open declaration that their ends can be achieved by the forceful overthrow of all existing social conditions. He is of the view that right end can never be achieved through wrong means. His firm conviction is that it is futile to preach religion among the downtrodden. We must remove their poverty and their suffering. Anand like Gandhi, gave a message of unity and harmony, friendship and co-operation. In Marx we find intolerance. But in Anand we find tolerance which is preached by Gandhi.

Anand is for the renewal of the decadent society. He thinks that the time is now ripe to have human protest, metaphysical protest, religious protest, social protest, etc., on all sides. Anand's protest is not destructive but creative. He dreams of human society totally sympathetic, compassionate, tolerant and utterly uninhibited in which every human being can find his full development physical, mental and aesthetic and can enjoy political, social, economical and other freedoms. He strives for a tolerant society where all are equal. Like the Buddha, he accepted the principles of Ahimsa. Violence has got no place in the teachings of Anand. He laid stress on purity of conduct, truthfulness, love and benevolence, charity and kindness and mercy to all living beings.

Concepts of 'man' and 'alienation' bring Anand closer to Marx. According to Marx, 'Man' under the capitalist set up is not really human, because "the Proletariat is a class that represents the complete loss of Man" (*Early writings*, pp. 137-139).

This dehumanization of man according to Marx, is due to his self-alienation under bourgeois order. Anand like Marx, believed in the Darwinian theory of evolution. According to Marx, capitalist system with classes, division of labour and money is the root cause of man's alienation. Marx's alienation theory can be termed as 'self realisation theory' according to some leading thinkers. Anand like Marx, was concerned with the problem of human alienation. Poverty has crushed the people and their individuality has been reduced to non entity. The working classes and the poor are alienated and Anand wanted to elevate the downtrodden and help them overcome their alienation. There seems to be an awakening in the minds of the downtrodden in realising their legitimate rights. A day will come when the shudra class rule over India.

Anand's concept of alienation is the consequence of a particular socio-economic system. He does not believe in the spiritual and non-material dimension of man. The soul's identification with the body and mind complex is the root cause of alienation. Anand is all for a change of socio-economic order in such a way that the neglected and exploited masses could regain their lost individuality, realise their full manhood, and overcome their age old sense of alienation and he is for the fullest development of man. The elimination of the feeling of alienation and the attainment of self realisation have been in consonance with Anand's philosophy.

Untouchable tends to emphasize the theme — man alienated from an absurd world, the individual estranged from society, the individual's isolation and subjectivity, his consequent feelings of anxiety, anguish, his assertion of personal freedom. *Untouchable* pictures the epic struggle of the individual Bakha to release himself from the communal customs and beliefs. There is a social conflict which results in the isolation of the individual from the society. The conflict between the society and the individual forces him to experience a type of 'self-exile'. Bakha's alienation is 'the result of social ostracism'. Anand has portayed Bakha as emerging from the old fatalism into a new road of freedom. Bakha learns the doctrine of struggle. He becomes a universal gesture of protest. He is persecuted by individuals as well as by society. He becomes a representative of the forces of modernity. Anand makes him strike rebellious postures. Aggression does not take the form of physical action or violence in the novel but it is there in the mind of Bakha. As he moves from one experience to another we can see the development of his mind which becomes more and more aggressive. He rebels inwardly against the exploitation but resigns to his lot. The segregated life that Bakha leads accompanied by miserable living conditions moulds him to protest. His aspiration for a decent life with good education has helped him break the bonds of slavery. There is a ray of hope seen in him when he returns home. In his preface E.M. Forster says :

> His Indian day is over and the next day will be like it, but on the surface of the earth if not in the depths of the sky, a change is at hand (101).

Anand thinks that only the change in socio-economic order will awake the exploited masses to regain their lost individuality to overcome their age old sense of alienation. In order to make changes in socio-economic order Anand thinks that the true nature of man, pity, compassion must be awakened not only in the working class but also in all. In order to arouse pity, compassion man must worship work. Work must be our religion. Bakha did not hate his job but he worshipped his work. He was sincere and duty conscious. He was happy and contented in working at the latrines. He was of the opinion that man has to work for the pay he received. He had a great devotion to duty.

> He went forward with eager step from job to job, a marvel of movement dancing through his work. Work was a sort of intoxication which gave him a glowing health and plenty of easy sleep (*UT*, 19).
>
> Bakha had principles. With him duty came first, although he was a champion of all kinds of games and would have beaten them hollow at Khuti. He seemed too intent on his work and he was going to move on (*UT*, 40).

The character of Bakha throws light on the humanistic ideals of work as worship and dignity of labour which are generally denied to men who do menial job by men doing white collar job.

Anand's choice of proletarian characters brings him close to Marx but his delineation of characters brings him close to the influence of Gandhi. Marx wants the characters to be pictured as the writers want them to be or as they should be. This can partially be applied to Bakha, the child of modern India who wants to lead a decent life and longs for fashion. Depiction of idealised reality is the motto of Marxian literature. In Anand we have both social realism and socialist realism. Bakha apes Western fashion and strives hard to lead a life of cleanliness. He is unlike a typical traditional sweeper. All other characters except Bakha are the reflections of Anand's real life observations. Other features of his novels follow this basic quality. This type of social realism is found in *Untouchable*. The suffering of Bakha delineated in the novel is the suffering of the untouchables. Religious hypocrisy is exposed realistically through the Sohini episode. This novel is based on the tradition of social realism. The picture of the outcaste's colony that we see even in the beginning of the novel is realistic.

Anand's concentration in presenting the tragic and inhuman plight of the lowest dregs of Indian society, the class struggle and the championing of the proletarian class tempts us call him a doctrinaire Marxist. His reaction towards Marx's 'Letter on India' clearly reveals that he has been greatly influenced by him. On reading this Anand wrote that the whole world was opened to him. He was able to visualise not only the history of India but also the whole history of the human society in some sort of interconnection. He thought that Marxism was a scientific and rational method for the study of society, a hypothesis which was leading to new discoveries.

Anand wrote *Untouchable* with a sense of social anger akin to Marxist's anger but later his contact with Gandhi, his reading of the magazine *Young India* and his realisation of Gandhi's attitude towards outcastes made him revise his novel. He retouched the novel with the same sense of love for the sweeper. Anand himself says, "I am sure, however, that the warmth towards Bakha which has made this character lovable to many people may, to some extent, have emerged from my warmth towards the person of Gandhi." The influence of Gandhi on the choice of the theme of untouchability is evident from the novel itself. Kai Nicholson says :

> The high point of the novel is when Gandhi speaks out against untouchability, but praises the humble origin of the untouchable making him a man of God and denouncing those who believe that because of his dharma a man is polluted and can pollute others. Thus the novel expresses ideas which are in alingnment with Mahatma Gandhi's on untouchability as a problem in the Hindu society.

Gandhi appears as a character towards the end of the novel *Untouchable* and speaks on the topic of the evil of untouchability. He wants an ideal Hindu society without any caste discrimination.

> A scavenger named Uka, an untouchable, used to attend our house for cleaning the latrines. Often I would ask my mother why it was wrong to touch him, and why I was forbidden to do. If I accidentally touched Uka, I was asked to perform ablutions; and though I naturally obeyed, it was not without smilingly protesting that untouchability was not sanctioned by religion and that it should be so. I was a very dutiful and obedient child; but so far as was consistent with respect for my parents. I often had arguments with them on this matter. I told my mother that she was entirely wrong in considering physical contact with Uka was sinful; it could not be sinful (*UT*, 161).

Mahatma Gandhi longs for a change of heart so that "All public wells, temples, roads, schools, sanitariums must be declared open to these untouchables (*UT*, 164).

The Mahatma seemed to have touched the most intimate corner of his soul (*UT*, 165).

The novel ends with the three possible solutions to the perennial problem of untouchability — Jesus Christ or conversion to Christianity, Mahatma Gandhi or the abolition of untouchability, the machine or the introduction of flush system. Bakha returns to his father thinking of the Mahatma, now of the machine. *Untouchable* ends on a note of inconclusiveness. There seems to be no definite and clear cut ending of the novel. Anand seems to leave the end of the novel in a state of uncertainty. According to Prof. Naik,

> *Untouchable* ends in an inconclusive note which is a mark of authenticity for an outcaste of the India of Nineteen thirties could only have been dimly conscious of possible solutions to his problem.

Anand does not clearly state his choice. The reformist zeal of Anand compels him to suggest ways and means to build a casteless society in which all will be equal.

Though Anand advocates Gandhian approach to untouchability, he does not endorse it. He seems to be in favour of machine which is clearly seen in the depiction of the poet who is the mouthpiece of Anand, the novelist.

Transformation of the world was the sole aim of Marx, Gandhi and Anand. Marx gave a revolutionary gospel to change the course of history and his philosophy was based on the concept of struggle for existence, class war and the concept of the survival of the fittest. Anand does not have faith in open rebellion. In Marx we find intolerance but in Anand we find tolerance which is the powerful weapon given by Gandhi. The young poet, the mouthpiece of Anand, in *Untouchable* criticises Gandhi's approach and suggests the introduction of flush system as the only solution to the problem of untouchability. Though Anand advocates Gandhian approach to untouchability as one of the possible ways of eradicating the practice of untouchability, he does not endorse it. He is not able to dissolve the Marxist and Gandhian approach. There seems to be a synthesis of Marxism and Gandhism in his novel *Untouchable.*

●

6

A Crusade Against Social Exploitation : Mulk Raj Anand's *Two Leaves and A Bud*

T. VASUDEVA REDDY

Mulk Raj Anand, a pioneer in the field of Indo-English fiction, has succeeded in carving for himself a special niche, and he is reverentially called one of 'The Big Three'. All his novels and short stories bear him out as a champion of the underdog and his writings reveal his deep understanding of socio-economic problems. No wonder, of all the Indian novelists in English, Anand is undoubtedly, a writer with a strong commitment to expose the social evils of inequity and exploitation, and as such he takes cudgels against the cruel forces and unsocial elements that relish the vicious pleasure of spreading the pall of dread over the lives of the poor. More often the criticism levelled against Anand is that he is the most 'committed' and 'propaganda' writer who champions the cause of the 'downtrodden and under-privileged' and that his writings reveal his Marxist disposition. It is really a matter of regret to note that for quite a long time due recognition was not accorded to him though he richly deserved it and that is the reason why Prof. C.D. Narasimhaiah once remarked that "Anand has not had his share of praise from the serious literary critic. He has been dubbed a social propagandist without being read and unfortunately the titles of his novels have had a good deal to do with the prevalent prejudice."[1]

The reason for this long neglect is probably on account of the lack of proper understanding and appreciation of Anand's thematic as well as moral concerns and the aesthetic dialectics in his novels in the perspective of the Indian sensibility. The problem becomes all the more critical because the Indian writer writing in English finds himself in the unpleasant situation of "using the English language in a way that will be distinctively Indian and still remains English."[2]

Fully conscious of this practical hurdle that lies across the path of the Indo-English novelist, Anand advises both his readers and critics to guard themselves against the danger of accepting totally the Western novel, for the novelist in Indian English has to "reveal the new consciousness of our old age people in all the miscellaneous, through the imaginative portrayal of human life that is the novel."[3] It is this difficulty that makes the critic's task rather critical, and as such the critic in Indian English has to frame his own tools afresh not only for evaluating the work but for arriving at a new type of criticism so as to suit to the changed context. In this situation Anand has the required talent to face the challenge by making use of the appropriate fictional strategies so as to imbue everything he writes with his essentially Indian ethos.

The eminence of Anand's fictional art lies in the realistic portrayal of the abject plight of the suffering masses and as such all his writings abound with the essential human sympathy. Jack Lindsay's perceptive essay refers to the "elements of deep human feeling and large-scale vision,"[4] on which his creative art is firmly established. All his writings enable us have a panoramic view of the rural life in India with all its merits and drawbacks and to a large extent they succeed in presenting a Kaleidoscopic range of Indian life, mostly the peasant life. His thorough knowledge of the masses and their plight gives him an added advantage in painting the peasant life with vividness of description and concreteness of detail. It is this photographic presentation that leads to the pervasive aspect of verisimilitude in his fiction and makes his fictional themes more appealing. Though the main characters such as Bakha in *Untouchable*, Munoo in *Coolie* or Gangu in *Two Leaves and a Bud* are his own powerful creations, they rise above the limited confines of the thematic sphere and strongly stand for a social cause.

Anand, being a true disciple of Gandhiji and having stayed with the latter at the Sabarmati Ashram, imbibed profound human values and as such he rebels at the irrational traditional ways and the cruel system of social exploitation and solemnly started a crusade against social exploitation. As such Novel becomes a potential instrument with which he could reform the society by laying bare all the ills and evils and by taking cudgels against social injustice. *Untouchable* (1935), *Coolie* (1936) and *Two Leaves and a Bud* (1937) are, in unequivocal terms, a crusade against the injustice done to the poor peasants and the lower classes by the upper classes in the caste dominant Indian society. *Untouchable* is an earnest expression of his moral indignation at the social injustice perpetrated by the traditional Hindu society on the lower classes, suppressed for generations. The writer has the basic moral courage to express his anger, and this moral courage is clearly discernible in the thematic selection as well as in the selection of the title. Moreover, the novel is a bold departure from the traditional one in the sense that he writes with a social purpose and makes a sweeper the central character.

Anand has seen the society in all its layers from all the angles and with his close knowledge of the living conditions of the sweepers, he creates the character of Bakha. The novel is about the life of an outcaste Bakha, a young sweeper living in the outcastes colony of a cantonment set in North India. The colony becomes the living symbol of the age-old practice of the sin of untouchability with pseudo-religious vigour. Bakha, being a sensible boy looks at the sordid situation with his rational mind, develops a feeling of loathsomeness at his miserable situation; and his tender heart is filled with indignant hatred at the caste Hindus when he is punished for accidentally touching a man in the street on the charge of polluting him. At a later stage the temple priest makes an attempt to molest his sister and when she rejects his advances, the debased priest vindictively accuses her on the charge of polluting him.

At the later stage, seeing a boy wounded while playing hockey with other boys in the cantonment, he carries him in his arms to his house when the boy's mother accuses him of injuring her son and polluting her house by his defiling touch. As the novel progresses, though he doesn't find any sign of hope towards a shadow of progress in his miserable situation, he gets three possible solutions to the problem from three different angles — from a missionary to become a Christian, from the inspiring speech of Gandhiji to fight out untouchability and from a young poet who suggests improved sanitation as the only way to drive out untouchability. At the end of the novel, Bakha is found 'thinking of everything he has heard, though he could not understand it all' (p. 133).

While Anand presents a realistic picture of the pitiable state of a social outcaste in the novel *Untouchable*, he now concentrates on the miserable condition of the labour class in his next two novels — *Coolie* and *Two Leaves and a Bud*. *Coolie* gives us a realistic account of an orphan Munoo who comes from the Kangra Hills and leaves the place in search of some work for his livelihood. First he joins as a servant in the house of a middle-class family in Sham Nagar, then moves to a pickle factory as a worker, later works as a coolie in the Bazaar at Daulatpur, later as a labourer in a cotton mill in Bombay and finally as a rickshaw puller in an Anglo-Indian household in Simla where the heaviness of the physical labour drains all his energy as a result of which he falls a prey to consumption and to an untimely death. Obviously the novel is an expression of the writer's protest against social exploitation of the poor landless peasant. "In his treatment of these themes," says M.K. Naik, "Anand's compassion for the underdog and his indignation at the exploitation of the Indian by the forces of capitalism, industrialism, communalism, colonialism and racism invest these two novels with a great power, so long as his artistic control over his material does not slacken."[5]

Anand's moral indignation at social injustice acquires greater momentum and stronger intensity in *Two Leaves and a Bud* than in his earlier novels and leaves a stronger impression on our minds. This novel is a faithful depiction of the theme of exploitation of the poor peasant on an elaborate scale and paints the class-conflict between the poor Indian workers in tea plantation and the owners of the tea plantation. The conflict is clearly between the rich and the poor, the exploiters and the exploited, the humble and the cruel forces, the natives and the foreigners; in other words it is a confrontation between the East and the West. It is this East-West encounter that makes the novel all the more powerful and it is this racial conflict that lends greater significance to the novel, while the thematic concern with exploitation makes it universal.

Gangu, the central character in the novel, is portrayed so realistically and convincingly that he draws our pity and sympathy from the beginning to the end. He can never be dishonest and deceitful and that is why he loses all his ancestral property in scrupulously clearing all the debts. At a time when he is in utter poverty, Sardar Buta tempts him to quit his village in the Punjab and follow him to the tea plantation though far away, with attractive promises such as the distribution of a plot of land free of cost, and obviously it is too powerful a temptation for a poor landless peasant to resist. But when he actually goes there with all the hope to the distant Macpherson Tea Estate in the Assam Valley, to his total disappointment he finds the place a virtual prison and the land so liberally promised turns out to be an elusive bait. The workers are so ill-paid that they are compelled to starve on many occasions and live ill-fed in unhealthy conditions; consequentially Gangu's wife falls ill and dies. De la Havre, the Young British doctor who pities the Indian labourers, gives a clear description of their miserable state in the novel :

> "These coolies didn't look as if they would require the breathing space of 700 cubic feet, or the floor area of 36 feet that an ordinary human being requires. And these heathens are the scum of the earth, who lived without any notion whatever of hygiene and sanitation... And, of course, slowly and surely, they must be taught the alphabet' (pp. 137-8).

The doctor becomes the mouthpiece of the writer whose pity is directed at the illiteracy and the ignorance, superstition and stupidity of the peasants or the rural folk.

The sad situation of the natives is presented against the backdrop of the British tyranny represented by the tea plantation. Native workers are treated worse than beasts by the British officials and the poor Indians seem to have mastered the art of suffering meekly with inferiority complex in the hands of the white imperialists who always feel powerful and superior to the sons of the soil. Craft-Cooke and Reggie Hunt, the British Asst. Manager of the tea-plantation represent the imperial British tyranny, and both of them seem to be totally devoid of human considerations and sympathy, for they treat workers as sub-human beings. They are always conscious of their power as well as their racial superiority which becomes a part of their blood. Wherever they go, they build Gothic structures for their luxurious residence and raise barns for the coolies. They never take the Indian workers into confidence and as such they magnify a quarrel between two women coolies into an uprising and take stern action. Gangu, after the death of his wife, is seen living only for his daughter. When Reggie Hunt, the depraved and unscrupulous Assistant Manager, tries to rape his daughter, he comes to her rescue and is shot dead. The irony of fate is such that Gangu, who comes all the way to the tea plantation at Assam to begin a new life, meets his abrupt death in the hands of the lecherous beast who literally hunts him and shoots him dead. The social protest reaches its climactic point when this human hunter is discharged when 'an impartial jury' has found him 'not guilty on the charge of murder and culpable homicide (p. 176). It is at this point that the novelist's crusade against social injustice becomes more emphatic, since even the jury, the so called custodians of justice, had hunted out justice from the tea plantation, which infact symbolically represents the human world at the micro level.

Profound humanism in Anand forces him to fight out the pronounced enemies of humanism — inequality and injustice, racial or economic — that reign supreme in the society. It is in this sense that the novel *Two Leaves and a Bud* is more or less a veritable chronicle narrating the novelist's crusade against social exploitation and injustice. Thus the novel as a whole is a faithful record of the tragic fate of a poor peasant who is rather callously denied of the fundamental right to minimum happiness, domestic as well as economic, at home and in the society. The novelist's humane sympathy for the oppressed and earnest human concern for the underdog invest the novel with a unique power that places him at a higher pedestal.

REFERENCES

1. C.D. Narasimhaiah, *The Journal of Commonwealth Literature* (Leeds), 1968.
2. Meenakshi Mukherjee, *The Twice Born Fiction*, New Delhi : Heinemann, 1971, p. 170.
3. Mulk Raj Anand, 'A note on Henry James and the Art of Fiction in India' *Commonwealth Quarterly*, Mysore, Vol. 122, No. 7, June 1978, p. 7.
4. Jack Lindsay, 'Mulk Raj Anand,' *Kakatiya Journal*, p. 2.
5. M.K. Naik, *Mulk Raj Anand*, New York : Humanities Press, 1973.

7

A Dark Drama of Exploitation : An Approach to *Two Leaves and A Bud*

K. SUNEETHA RANI

Mulk Raj Anand has always written to emphasise the essential dignity of man, despite his weaknesses, and to engender compassion in the hearts of the readers for the oppressed and the downtrodden. His literary life has been an incessant struggle, characterised by an intrepid protest against inhumanity and a boundless compassion for man. Tenderness is the essence of Anand's humanism. In his own words, "I hope I can teach even a few people of my generation that tenderness is our only asset."[1] His chief preoccupation is with the people without land or with little land condemned to starvation and to seasonal or permanent emigration. His peasants are loaded with debt and disease, harvesting little grain but reaping a prolific crop of troubles all the year round. He is righteously indignant that the land is not of the whole nation but has been mostly usurped by a handful of the privileged. In his 'Introduction to Meet My People' Mulk Raj Anand says, "it is time that the half-dead ryot, kicked about by the Rajah and spat upon by the Bania, began to hit back."[2]

This problem of peasantry is portrayed in Anand's novel *Two Leaves and A Bud* in such a way as to project those aspects of the class struggle of Indian society which spell needless misery, hardship and unhappiness, aspects which need to be interpreted in terms of the conflict between pragmatic egoism and the socio-political necessity. This obsession with the problem of class system is traceable to Mulk Raj Anand's liberal humanism and his passionate commitment for the cause of the dispossessed. This novel is most effective as a piece of implied indictment.

Two Leaves and A Bud portrays the yawning hiatus between haves and have-nots, the rulers and the ruled, the exploiters and the exploited. The problem of class is a universal phenomenon. Mulk Raj Anand's interest lies in exploring the stresses and strains generated in Indian society as a result of the developing economic structure, expanding commerce and political change which necessarily demand new class arrangements in the society. His projection of the play of class-consciousness is distinguished by his extraordinary insight into the attitudes and the new responses of life which it has evoked.

The novel centres round the predicament of the working class or the underprivileged. The novelist with an unerring instinct charts the course of life governed by the hydraheaded capitalist system of exploitation. *Two Leaves and A Bud* presents the tribulations of the coolies in a class-ridden society as a group experience in the framework of a vast capitalistic organisation. It is about the family of a helpless peasant Gangu lured off to the world of Assam plantations, which is too dense a jungle for the ray of love to penetrate. He migrates on the false promises of a clever coolie-catcher. Gangu experiences endless humiliations and dies at the hands of his unscrupulous boss.

The novel starts with the cliche of Indian philosophy : 'Life is like a journey.' Though life is a journey, the poor man's life is the most unhappy journey. There are no delightful resorts on the way and the destination of the journey is also not a heaven but a hell. They travel from sorrow to sorrow, exploitation to exploitation, to use Samuel Beckett's phrase, 'from nothingness to nothingness.' It is an unconscious journey towards eternal doom. It is a journey straight into the mouth of Hell. Gangu travels never to return.

Gangu's pleasant home in Hoshiarpur is seized by the Government saying that as the brothers hold joint property, his brothers' debt should be incurred by Gangu. "Strange," Gangu thinks, "how the interest on my younger brother's mortgage piled up, so that all my three acres and my hut as well just as a free gift to Seth Badri Das."[3] Left with no other choice, Gangu leaves the village.

The promised paradise of plenty with its thick vegetation and idyllic greenery is only a mirage. It is a profound 'morbid dystopia.'

> He (Prem's father) never talked to her in that manner on a footing of equality and comradeship. Her study abroad had given a new dimension to her personality and her father apparently noticed it and accepted it. She was very happy to be received by her father as a participant in his intellectualism (45-46).

What the novelist thinks is "if people who have gone abroad come back and serve the country, a new outlook may prevail" (93). And the novelist appears to speak through Lal, who on the verge of leaving for India, expresses his noble sentiments thus :

> "We come here for a short stay. We see new things. We receive new ideas. But we have to go back and serve our country" (26).

Another evil, the novelist takes up for censure is the caste system in the Indian society. When Ravi writes to his father, Ramesam about his intension to marry Prem, a woman from a different caste, his father declines to give his assent for it. This surprises Ravi as his father, a Gandhian and freedom fighter, is known for his social reform. What Ravi does not understand is that his father has lost much of his property in his selfless service to the country. In his old age, Ramesam pinned all his hopes on Ravi, the eldest of his five children to support the financially crippled family. Accordingly he desires that Ravi should marry a woman from an affluent family but one from his own caste. As he grows older, he becomes more conventional and does not possess courage to oppose social prejudices and practices. So it is convenient for him to dismiss the whole affair as infatuation and suggests that there are equally intelligent and educated girls in their own caste. He "... talked of traditional values and attitudes towards life and how each caste would cherish and nourish its own culture and customs zealously" (27).

When Ravi returns to India and visits the village, he realises how heavily they are in debt. Though he is torn between his loyalty for his father and his loyalty for Prem, he realises that his independent spirit will never allow him to be sold for dowry to the highest bidder. Ramesam, realising that what Ravi has for Prem is not infatuation but real love comes round and approves Ravi's marriage with Prem. He only says :

> "Ravi, you are free to marry anyone you like. But only choose the right one. That's all I would like to say in this matter" (75).

Thus, Ravi's romantic love transcends communal and social barriers. Through the love story of Ravi and Prem, the novelist seems to give a message to the people that :

> Conventions and traditions are after all man made for the convenience and comfort of society. Once they do not serve that purpose we should discard them, not hang on to them (28-29).

The novelist's exhortation to the Indians abroad not to belittle their motherland in the eyes of the foreigners seems to be similar to the poetic utterance of Sri Rayaprolu Subbarao. Ravi, who is every inch an Indian, supports everything that is Indian. He knows that he can be critical of India in India, but outside the country, whatever may be its limitations, it is his duty to defend it from the jeering remarks of the others. That is why, at a dinner hosted by the Drama Society in Denver, he acts as an un-official ambassador of his country, stoutly championing his country, defending the policies of Gandhiji and Nehru and infact everything that is Indian. He often dreams that one day his country too possessing all natural resources, would be as rich as America. He imagines a state of blissful prosperity for his country. As an engineer, he thinks it is his duty to :

> Build mighty bridges and dams, tame the Indian rivers, control the floods and bring prosperity to the teeming millions of the country (40).

Through Ravi, the novelist expresses his urge that every Indian should love his country earnestly. It is the novelist speaking through Ravi, when he says :

> I have a commitment to the country. I feel that every Indian who comes here for higher studies should go back and serve his country (34).

Through Ramesam and Ravi, the novelist, perhaps, suggests that in the pre-independence India, the country required Ramesam like Congressmen who were prepared for any kind of sacrifice to free the Country from alien rule. Nationalism, commitment to work, sacrifice and such recognised Indian qualities are becoming rare now. The independent India requires people like Ravi with enormous love for the country. So, the novelist fervently appeals, to the Indian intellectuals abroad, through his spokesman, Ravi. to "... look homeward and help the nation" (93).

Commenting on the message the novel conveys, K.R. Srinivasa Iyengar aptly remarks that the novel has a 'pointed relevance for India.'[4] Even two decades after the publication of the novel, the message still has relevance to the contemporary Indian Society. It should, however, be said to Rama Sarma's credit that his attitude towards life is not negative. He believes that a novel is not merely to depict the problems of life but to suggest solutions too. He looks forward to social change and in that pursuit presents an optimistic and affirmative picture. His solutions may sound romantic and idealistic to some extent. However, they reflect the novelist's deep sense of love for and commitment to his country.

REFERENCES

1. Leo Lowenthal, *Literature and the image of Man*, Boston : Beacon Press, 1957, p. 3.
2. G. Nageswara Rao, 'M.V. Rama Sarma', edited by Madhu Sudan Prasad, *Indian English Novelists*, New Delhi : Sterling Publishers, 1982, p. 109.
3. Rama Sarma, *Look Homeward*, Madras : Blackie & son, 1976, p. 25. All further page references are to this edition and are incorporated in the text of the article.
4. Quoted from a letter from Prof. K.R. Srinivasa Iyengar to Prof. Rama Sarma, dated 3-3-1976.

15

Sociological Values in Romen Basu's Rural Novels

P. SOMANATH

Romen Basu has definite views about the nature and purpose of fiction. He declares :

> Fiction is a human document. For me, unless it has some bearing on real life it cannot to taken seriously as a work of creation.[1]

He admits that he is influenced 'a great deal' by Mulk Raj Anand. However, he denies writing novels with a social purpose like Anand and Bhattacharya. "That is Why," he says "I have not accepted having been described as a sociological novelist."[2] However, this appears to be an understatement as his novels bear immense sociological value.

Romen Basu's three rural novels (1) *The Tamarind Tree* (1975), (2) *Outcast* (1986) and (3) *Blackstone* (1989) could be seen as novels with a specific social purpose. They are aimed at presenting the social and economic problems of rural Bengal with a view to forging social reform and a just and equitable social order. Among them, *The Tamarind Tree* is the most satisfying in terms of the theme and its execution besides characterization.

The Tamarind Tree seeks to present in fictional terms the success of a village girl, Mohamaya, in helping "to bring a smile or two in the midst of misery"[3] in the village, Balavpur, in an unobtrusive, unassuming, selfless and non-violent way and in bringing about peace, unity and communal harmony. Romen Basu appears to understate Mohamaya's quiet confidence and fearless crusade against the evils of the village life in India and calls for a similar crusade and passion to cleanse the village life, for the roots of India are in its villages. The novel is an affirmation of Gandhian values such as Hindu-Muslim unity, prohibition, removal of untouchability and, above all, non-violent approach to social problems. Hence, the immense relevance of the novel.

The implicit social purpose of the novel seems to show how the evils of the village life can be cleansed in a non-violent way. Romen Basu presents the rural social conditions with a keen sense of realism. The main plot consisting of Mohamaya's role in the village affairs and the subplot consisting of Anukul's property affairs are fused and Balavpur remains the scene of action for both the main plot and the subplot. The fictional focus rests on the character of Mohamaya, the daughter of the village headmaster. A reviewer says :

> She has grown up in the village and was a strange child from the start, a little St. Bright with an uncontrollable tendency to make fast friends among the social, political and religious groups, the castes and outcastes that are so variegated even in a small plot of India.[4]

Mixing with the untouchables has been her habit since her childhood. For Mohamaya, Balavpur is her world. Her identification with the people and their problems is total and she is consistent in her attachment to them throughout the novel. The city-bred Biren is charmed by her courage, straightforwardness and convictions. As he comes into closer contact with her, he finds her unusual in her tastes and opinions. She sees that caste barriers have made people small-minded. She asserts that "even if they kill me, I will not discriminate between people."[5]

Aversion to city life is another major trait of her personality. After her marriage with Biren, she is forced to live in Calcutta. She finds herself unable to adjust to the prejudice and snobbery inside and outside Biren's family. The imitation of Western culture is too hard for her to put up with. She feels sick at the food and dance in the night club. She finds "the distance between Balavpur and Calcutta as a gulf too wide to be bridged."[6] Calcutta cannot "touch her soul which always flutters for her people in the village."[7] Paramanik, a barber from Balavpur goes to see her and narrates the deteriorating conditions at Balavpur such as the Hindu-Muslim factions, blackmarket operations, lawlessness, atrocities of money-lenders and selfish contractors, drought and so on. He tells her that "within a year none of the old villagers would be found in Balavpur unless someone could help them"[8] and requests her to "come and see us before half of us are dead."[9] Mohamaya thinks that she is responsible for the conditions. She decides to go back to Balavpur to set things right. At Balavpur, she uses her goodwill with the Muslim leader, Bakshi and shows skill, persuasion, and diplomacy in avoiding a Hindu-Muslim conflict. She pleads for unity among all castes of Hindus. Mohamaya's success with Bakshi is a starting point for the easing of many tensions in the village. Summing up her triumphs, a reviewer says :

> Without being too explicit in her methods, Mohamaya could handle almost all rural problems, heal differences between caste Hindus and the untouchables and between Hindus and Muslims by sheer will power that transcends her own personal happiness.[10]

Mohamaya's dream is fulfilled as Biren comes to Balavpur to stay with her. She is one of the rare women characters in Indian fiction in English and is hailed as "Basu's most thoughtful creation."[11] She is a shining example of the virtues, strength and wisdom of Indian womanhood.

Thus, *The Tamarind Tree* calls for a 'belief in the village' and demonstrates the victory of forces of unity over forces of disintegration. The novel is also an affirmation of 'the values of village life.' One feels that it is with justification it has been called "the finest of Basu's novels" and "one of the best contributions to Indo-English fiction from Bengal."[12]

Like *The Tamarind Tree*, Romen Basu's second rural novel, *Outcast* (1986), stands out as a novel of social purpose. Set in rural West Bengal, the novel deals with the lonely war that Sambal, an untouchable wages against an unjust and oppressive society and his estrangement from individuals and groups — Putki the girl who loves him, Parashar, the progressive teacher who supports him, and the communists who want to make use of him. The novel presents a vivid picture of a Bengali village, Basuli, and the divisions that split not only the high-caste from the low, but the various gradations of the untouchables which prevent them from coming together to fight oppression. It is also an effective expose of the complexities of political organizing in rural India. While *The Tamarind Tree* ends on a note of hope, *Outcast* ends in gloom and despair.

As in *The Tamarind Tree*, the purpose of the novelist is to present the evils of rural society and the efforts to bring about social change. We may say that, like Mulk Raj Anand's first three novels — *Untouchable*, *Coolie* and *Two Leaves and a Bud* — Basu's novel abounds in social realism. A reviewer says :

> The novel is cast just after India won her independence : but surprisingly writing in 1986, Romen Basu manages to capture the present-day life and the ethos in which the untouchable still lives today... The untouchable is still scared of the upper caste : he still lives in humiliation; and he ekes out a miserable existence at the mercy of the upper caste.[13]

The novel is a fine sympathetic portrayal of Indian reality in terms of the lives of the dispossessed. The author incorporates many instances of social, economic, political and religious exploitation of the low-castes in the course of the narrative and one feels that a gloomy and sinister picture is painted. The social system, as presented in the novel, is afflicted with inhuman division and distorted values.

The former zamindar, Paramesh Ganguli, symbolizes the social and economic exploitation of the low-caste people in the village, Basuli. He is the embodiment of social bigotry and resentment for the low-caste people. Their children are not allowed in school. They should not use tube wells. Medicine is denied to them in the dispensary. He instigates the high-caste people to assault Sambal's father physically because he is an 'untouchable' and has entered the Kali temple. Further, the low-caste people are subjected to economic exploitation. The zamindar pays the lowest daily rate and anyone who demands better wages is beaten ruthlessly. He has forcibly occupied hundreds of acres of land which belongs to poor peasants. Labourers are squeezed to starvation.

Sambal is the symbol of resistance against casteism and economic exploitation symbolized by Paramesh Ganguli. His father's humiliation makes him, even as a boy, permanently embittered and he grows up to be an angry young man. He is obsessed with the idea of revenge on an unjust society. As he grows, his motive for revenge transforms into fiery idealism. Sambal's evolution as a revolutionary may be studied in three stages — first, his career till the Gram Panchayat is formed, second, his association with communists and the subsequent disillusionment with them, and third, the phase of his self-isolation.

Sambal realizes that his revenge on Paramesh and on the caste system is possible only by uniting the untouchables cutting across their caste differences and preparing an organization. He is supported by Manmatha, the Communist leader, from whom Sambal learns how to organize his supporters. But, to his dismay and despair, Sambal fails to obliterate the caste differences among the untouchables. He is further disillusioned by Manmatha's change of stance as directed by the Communist Party. Manmatha defers the issue of forging equality among the untouchables. Sambal accuses Manmatha of hypocrisy. The construction of a Shiva temple by Paramesh for the untouchables leads to a clash between the two untouchable castes — the Bagdis and the Muchis — over the management of the temple. The Bagdis refuse Sambal's plea to share the powers with other untouchables so that the temple becomes an expression of equality among them. Sambal accuses the Bagdi leader of opportunism for which he is bashed up and imprisoned. Thus, Sambal's chief motive of taking revenge on Paramesh Babu is overshadowed by his vain struggle to unite the low-castes as a first stop.

The phase of self-isolation in Sambal's career begins after his release from jail. He refuses reconciliation with Manmatha because the Communist Party shows no concern for 'the misery of the minority.' He also differs from Manmatha on the mode of bringing unity among the untouchables. While Manmatha insists on persuasion, Sambal wants to use force against Bagdis to take control of the temple and to bring equality among untouchables. He also insists on a plan of conducting marriages between the lower castes to bring about social intercourse for which, unfortunately, they are not prepared. He says he "will organise a group like a Naxalbari to achieve quick result."[14] Sambal is warned that he is only 'bent on self-destruction' if he demands this 'iron-clad understanding' by forming his own group. He wants to blow up the

Shiva temple. He even refuses to marry Putki as he has set his objective above his own life and personal pleasures. Putki commits suicide out of despair.

Like Mulk Raj Anand's *Untouchable*, Romen Basu's novel seems to have been written with a social purpose. It warns "against the perpetuation of caste system to its logical extreme, and the inevitable disaster."[15] The relevance of the novel lies in its implicit plea for social change. Thus, in *Outcast* Basu has put together "a diverse set of characters and woven a story that reads well, sound very true to life, invites compassion for the dispossessed and deprived, and makes its point with telling effect."[16]

Romen Basu's third rural novel, *Blackstone* (1989), deals with the armed peasant uprising in Debra-Gopibalavpur in West Bengal under Naxalite or Maoist leadership twenty years ago. The novel also draws the reader's attention forcefully to the 'angry conscience' of the oppressed peasants giving rise to the violent movement against exploitation and holds lessons for a just and equitable social order. In this sense, *Blackstone* and *Outcast* show great resemblances. As the blurb says, the author 'seeks to go beyond the images of violence that dominated the news media or the period to the human hurt and need behind it.' The author gives fictional treatment to the emergence of armed revolution to wipe out oppression, the setbacks faced and overcome by the revolution and the attempts to revive the revolution with a view to winning political power.

The story of Kalapathor forms the nucleus of the novel. His father, Karan, is harassed by the landlord, Gour Haldar, who demands his share of crop even when there are no rains. Karan pays with his life for informing the police of the illegal felling of sal trees by Gour Haldar's men.

Kalapathor becomes a vagabond. His sister is raped and killed by the police. When the novel opens, he is twenty, living on hunting and 'a tormented man, unable to forget the injustices his family had suffered.'[17] He is one among hundreds of landless peasants in Gopibalavpur district 'burning with passion to find justice for his fellowmen.' They repose faith in the Naxalite party Chairman in realizing their dream to have their own land. Initially, they succeed in killing a few landlords including Gour Haldar. The tempo of violence picks up when the students join the revolutionaries. The massacre of more than two hundred revolutionaries by the police puts the leaders on the defensive. Differences set in the Naxalite organization over the future course of action. By the end of the novel, the revolutionaries in the district sort out their differences and resolve to start a 'new struggle' with a renewed commitment to revolution.

Thus, from *The Tamarind Tree* to the third rural novel, *Blackstone*, Basu presents a steady progression from non-violence as the means of social reform to full-scale violence as the means of establishing a just social and economic order. In other words, Romen Basu seems to send a signal through the rural novels that a solution for the sundry problems of rural India need not necessarily be tainted with blood and that non-violent methods are in fact more effective in producing lasting results.

NOTES AND REFERENCES

1. Romen Basu's letter dated May 19, 1992.
2. *Ibid.*
3. Romen Basu, *The Tamarind Tree*, Calcutta : Writers Workshop, 1975, p. 218. All further references are to this edition.
4. Betty Kelen, rev. of *The Tamarind Tree*, *Trans India*, p. 1.
5. *The Tamarind Tree*, p. 51.
6. *Ibid.*, p. 140.
7. Jogendra Saksena, rev. of *The Tamarind Tree*, *National Herald*, August 22, 1976.
8. *The Tamarind Tree*, p. 154.
9. *Ibid.*, p. 155.
10. "Rural Cameos," rev. of *The Tamarind Tree*, *Sunday Standard*, September 26, 1976.
11. K.T., Krishna Prasad, "Romen Basu," *Indian English Novelists*, edited by Madhusudan Prasad, New Delhi : Sterling Publishers, 1982, p. 177.
12. *Ibid.*, p. 176.
13. Veena Singh : "Reality and Revolution?" rev. of *Outcast*, *Indian Book Chronicle*, May-June, 1987, p. 151.
14. Romen Basu, *Outcast*, New Delhi : Sterling Publishers, 1986, p. 235.
15. Anand Raj Singh, "Novel with a Social Purpose," rev. of *Outcast*, *The Pioneer*, May 10, 1987.
16. Shakuntala Narasimhan, "Shadows in the Countryside," rev. of *Outcast*, *Indian Express*, April 5, 1987.
17. Romen Basu, *Blackstone*, New Delhi : Sterling Publishers, 1989, p.3.

16

Self-assertion of Woman : Shashi Deshpande's *Roots and Shadows*

K.V. RAGHUPATHI

Loneliness, one of the concerns of Existentialists, is not merely an incorrigible disease but a symptom of modern man's predicament and the awareness of this has made him search for the true meaning of life. Ironically, the search itself has become a disease and meaningless and man has been eternally condemned to be free in the vicious circle of struggles. For long, woman in India and in other societies has been seeking an identity, and trying to declare that she is just a being and can live in the world where men also live. In trying to carve out a place for herself, she has become more and more self-assertive and cognitive of her position and rights. Modern woman's position and her predicament in the society are the same as those of man's, and her efforts and pursuits to extricate herself from her wretched and sordid position and confusion and carve out a place for herself in the men dominated society have further worsened her state. As a result, she suffers from loneliness more than her compeers in the past. Her constant search for self-autonomy and freedom has proved otherwise self-deceptive, horrendous and meaningless.

Shashi Deshpande's novels are mainly concerned with the self-assertion and loneliness of woman. Her chief concern is the human relations, not the rationalised but felt, perceived and real, not the traditional but redefined human relations, especially the relationship between man and woman. In all these the central figure is woman. For her writing the novel is life. She says "ultimately fiction is life-imagination. Imagination superimposing upon life, reshaping it.

Tidying it, creating some kind of an order out of the chaos. But you start with life. Imagination comes later. Life is the springboard."[1] Apart from this affirmation she has not spelt out her goal or purpose overtly anywhere.

Woman is the central object of her fiction. Her women characters are born out of a typically Indian situation. They represent middle-class society. Her theory is not the theory of Western feminism. In fact, she has no theories; she rejects them and she gives her own assessment of the predicament of Indian woman caught between tradition and modernity, between family and profession, between culture and nature, between assertion and confrontation, between freedom and loneliness, between self-aggrandisement and self-realization. The problems and conflicts faced by women in her novels are existential in nature. They occur for any woman in the society. Their self-assertion is self-alienation. The more the search for freedom and independence and the meaning of life, the more it results in alienation and loneliness. This is the typical of an existential problem every man encounters, and every modern woman according to Deshpande is facing. Deshpande, however, takes pity in her women characters for the predicament created by themselves through self-delusions and hallucinations; and towards the end she provides a touch of humanism mixed with love.

Deshpande has written six novels altogether. They are : *The Dark Holds No Terrors* (1980), *Come Up and Be Dead* (1983), *Roots and Shadows* (1983), *If I Die Today* (1982), *That Long Silence* (1988) and her last novel being *Binding Vine* (1993). All these novels deal with the middle-class women of Indian situation, their disharmony in their sexual, cultural and natural roles. These women are educated, sophisticated, married, intelligent, bold, assertive, independent and familiar with the problems of changing world and life. *Roots and Shadows* (1983), published after *The Dark Holds No Terrors* (1980), represents the woman's quest for identity, freedom and independence. The novel is remarkable for its exploration of the inner psyche. Indu, the protagonist, always wants to be free and independent. She works towards that, but fails at the end and strikes a compromise to the old traditional life.

The novelist uses the cinematic technique of flashback for

narration and the novel opens with Indu, middle-class orthodox Brahmin girl, returning to her ancestral place after eleven years in order to attend the funeral ceremony of Akka, the 'old rich family tyrant.' Akka, the surrogate mother of Indu, is a domineering woman in the novel. She is a childless widow and symbolises authority. Her word is a law in the house and no one dared to object and question her authority. Till her death, 'She had maintained her power, her authority over everyone.' Indu has been brought up under her authority and control. But she always questions her authority and wants to set herself free. Both Akka and Indu have incompatible temperaments and they represent two different worlds. Akka represents old generation, tradition and authority, while Indu new generation, modernity and freedom.

Indu finds her surrogate mother dominant and a hindrance to her freedom. At every stage she feels she is stifled and thwarted. She comes to the place to find her original roots and much to her distress discovers dark shadows falling on her life. When she studies in the college, Akka doesn't allow her to meet the boys and cultivate friendship with them. We find in the novel Indu leaving her home full of hatred for family, for Akka especially and she swears 'I would never go back' (20). Thus, she rebels against Akka's authority, world and her values and marries Jayant and enters another house to be independent and complete. This is the first step in her self autonomy.

In her married life, Indu wants to be more assertive and autonomous. She becomes possessive and always wants her husband Jayant to be with her. She observes : "When I look in the mirror, I think of Jayant, when I dress I think of Jayant, when I undress I think of him. Always what he wants, what he would like, what would please him. And I can't blame him. It is not he who has me into this. It is the way I want it to be... Have I become fluid, with no shape, no form of my own" (54). In this way she expresses her love for Jayant which has no limits, and she realizes that she is in no way different from others.

Indu thinks that marriage has given her freedom, but ironically enough, soon she realizes the futility of her decision. She says, "I wish I could say we have achieved complete happiness, But I can't fantasize" (14). She speaks about her own incompleteness thus :

"This is my real sorrow that I can never be complete in myself. Until I had met Jayant, I had not known it... that was somewhere outside me, a part of me without which I remained incomplete. Then I met Jayant and lost the ability to be alone" (34). She realizes : "I had learnt to reveal to Jayant nothing but what he wanted to see... I hide my responses as if they were bits of garbage" (41). The paradox is she is not happy with Jayant, but at the same time, she cannot live without him. She thinks she has achieved independence and completeness, but soon she realizes that her independence is not complete and total. She is not content, she wants something more.

Indu, like Saru in *The Dark Holds No Terrors* experiences disillusionment in sex and falls a victim of "sexual paralysis."[2] This silent sexual humiliation leads Indu to have extra marital relationship with Naren. This is the second step to express her self-autonomy. Both Indu and Saru seek freedom not only intellectually but sexually too. What is significant is that both Indu and Saru suffer from no guilt and they begin to evolve a new code of sexual ethics that suits their fantasies. Both the heroines undergo a new experience. Both give a new expression through extra marital sexual relationship. Both give a new interpretation of "love." Saru in *The Dark Holds No Terrors* reveals : "Love ... there was no such thing between man and woman... Only a need which both fought against futilely, the very futility owing into the thing called love" (65). Equally, Indu laughs at the idea of "love." "I love a book, a word, or a sari, a curry, a dog, a child, a man" (97). When Naren asks her what the truth is, she answers : "The sexual instinct... That is true. The material instinct... that is true too. Self interest, self love... they are the basic truths, you remember Devdas? I saw it with some friends. They sobbed when he died for love, but I could have buked. A grown man moaning and crying for love. God! A grown man moaning and crying for love. God! how disgusting!" (173). She thought that marriage would bring her freedom, but to her great shock and surprise, she found that Jayant had not only expected her to submit but had taken her submission for granted and she also, without being aware of it, submitted herself to him step by step in the name of love. She found it was not love but an adjustment as she never wanted conflict in her married life. As it was a love-marriage she did not want to give an impression to her parents that she had committed a mistake. She otherwise wanted to prove her success. She says pathetically : The hideous ghost of my own cowardice confronted me as I thought of this... that I had clung tenaciously to Jayant, to my marriage, not for love alone, but because I was afraid of failure, I had to show them that my marriage, that I, was a success... And so I went on lying, even to myself (115).

Thus, we see that both Saru and Indu realize that love has no place in the world; they see only deceit, treachery and hypocrisy. They also see that sex becomes a symbol of power and authority and marriage. Even in the second world of autonomy, both Indu and Saru realize that the extra-marital relationship is false, deceptive and misleading. They begin to understand that marriage has failed to satisfy their hunger for total independence. Marriage demands enormous sacrifice from woman and in that sacrifice she cannot express herself to be totally free and independent. In fact, a fresh bondage begins. In this way, both Indu and Saru become self-disillusioned in marriage and extra-marital relationship. Indu's quest for completeness turns out to be her quest for meaning for self and life.

After realizing her failure, Indu returns to her place and stays with Akka till the house is disposed off. Her return to the house is not another step into autonomy, but she becomes a refuge and starts introspecting deeply over her past life, her secret passions and sexual explorations. She learns from Akka more about her past, her concern, her suffering and her traumatic married life which resulted in the death of her husband. It is here Indu learns to be a little self-realized not in the mystical sense and she learns not to judge others by her standards. It is here that she realizes what her roots are, what her freedom is, what her moral responsibility is, her relationship in complex situations, and her different roles. There is a reconciliation in herself, though it is against the philosophy of existentialism.

There is a compromise to the tradition. She sees a fresh light in life. She takes a firm decision regarding her job and life : There were other things I had to tell him (Jayant). That I was resigning my job. That I would at last do the kind of writing I had always dreamt of doing. That I would not, could not enrich myself with Akka's money. That I would, on the other hand, pay for Mini's wedding

(205). This reconciliation and compromise contradict her deep longing for freedom, her struggles and pursuits. One does... not understand why the novelist has depicted Indu as a typical rebellious middle-class woman in the beginning and at the same time towards the end made her compromise with tradition. It appears as though the tragedy of Indu is quite evident, inevitable and inescapable. The struggle is eternal, and the anguish is irresistible. One also sees loneliness and misery in her search for freedom and identity.

For Indu the ancient house itself is a bondage and trap. She says, "as a matter of fact, I felt neither mournful, nor desolate, but in a peculiar way, both light and free. Yes, the house had been a trap too, binding me to a past I had to move away from. Now, I felt clean, as if I had cut away all the unnecessary uneven edges of me" (204). Also, the most striking quality is that Indu learns to see her life independent of Jayant. She is least concerned about her extra-marital relationship. She does not want to tell Jayant about it. That had nothing to do with the two of us and our life together.

There is an awareness of the futility of her autonomy and yet she realizes that she is a being, and not a dependent on Jayant. The novel ends in affirmation of the individuality of Indu and also the principle of life which is endless. She has learnt to see not only her life full of possibilities for growth and grace but the very meaning of life itself. "I felt as if I was watching life itself... endless, limitless, formless and full of grace'' (202). It is with this understanding, realization and reconciliation, she goes back to Jayant. She also realizes that Akka is not a sadist.

Though the novel gains its feminist stance, it goes beyond the limits of feminism and touches the very predicament of human existence. Though Deshpande provides 'the compromise attitude' for Indu towards the end, the whole novel deals with the existential dilemma of a typical modern middle-class woman. The existential trauma, conflict and anguish faced by Indu in the novel can be ascribed to any woman in the society. It is this beautiful presentation of the inner psyche of woman by Deshpande that can deeply impress any one in society.

REFERENCES

1. R.K. Dhawan, ed. *Indian Woman Novelists*, Vol. V, p. 34.
2. R. Mala, "*The Predicament of the Indian Women : The Heroines in the Novels of Shashi Deshpande : A Select Study*, M. Phil, Dissertation, Pondicherry University, 1989, p. 132.

All textual quotations are taken from Shashi Deshpande's *Roots and Shadows*, published by Orient Longman, 1983.

17

Life Inside the Cage : Shashi Deshpande's *That Long Silence*

G. LAKSHMI NARASAIAH

In her novel *That Long Silence* (1988) Shashi Deshpande tells us the story of man and woman from woman's point of view and of wife and husband from the wife's point of view. She describes and dissects the life inside the cage, behind the veil, under the bell jar from precisely that vantage point of inner space, the space most important to the existentialists. Through the depiction of Jaya's oppressed and unsatisfactory life, Shashi Deshpande has conveyed existential themes of absurdity of existence and nausea. In a tormenting saga of a tormented wife, the novelist portrays a search for authenticity. "The book is sprung with tension from start to finish. Jaya is incessantly ravelled by inner conflict, given to copious weeping, constantly analysing her oppressed lot in a male oriented society" (Walsh 1990 : 117). Gradually Jaya is affected by the idea of being a non-entity, of the irrationality of existence with a sense of excitement, fear and nausea. She starts "laughing at everything-marriage, as this whole absurd exercise we call life" (Deshpande 1988 : 122). She experiences a sense of anguish, a generalized uneasiness, a fear or dread. Ultimately the readers are made to think that "all existence is merely contingent, without any necessity to exist, without any rationality, any essence simply in the way, superfluous, de trop, and so it is absurd" (Lavine 1984 : 346).

The novel is shrewdly presented by Shashi Deshpande as Jaya's own series of memories, a first person account of both her past and present life, written only for herself, and thus as a direct and truthful statement on one woman's introspective analysis, her concrete existence. In evoking 'the original gushing forth of existence' Sashi Deshpande renders a spell-inducing tale not in the complete naturalistic style but with some magical realism we have come to associate with Gabriel Garcia Marquez, filling her protagonist's world with ghosts and luscious imagery that suggests meaning hidden even in the most ordinary things. In her 'Beloved' Toni Morrison has done the same thing.

Before her marriage, Jaya has been taught the importance of the husband in the life of women. Vanitamami tells her that 'a husband is a sheltering tree'. Ramukaka reminds her of the thing that the happiness of her husband and home depends entirely on her. When Jaya is leaving home after her marriage, Dada has advised her to 'be good to Mohan'. The women in Mohan's family have been a revelation to her. They are so definite about their roles, so well trained in their duties, so skilful in the right areas, so indifferent to everything else. Jaya has never seen a clear, so precise a pattern before, and she has been entranced by it. She tries to pattern herself after these women. That way gives her, if not happiness, atleast the consciousness of doing right, freedom from guilt. So, when something is not done well, or on time, a button missing, or a meal cooked badly, or too delayed, she has cringed in guilt. And when she has been praised for anything, she has been so ridiculously pleased. At the same time, she has her knowledge of Mohan, of his convictions : "A husband and wife care for each other, live with each other until they are dead; parents care for their children, and children in turn look after their parents where they are needed; marriages never end, they cannot — they are a state of being" (Deshpande 1988 : 127).

Enmeshed this way in the Indian family system, Jaya has lost her authenticity as a human being. She has shaped herself to the wishes of Mohan. She has given up the job she wanted to take, the baby she wanted to adopt and the anti-price campaign she had wanted to take part in. Since Mohan accuses her of not caring about the children, of isolating herself from him and his concerns, she has stopped her writing. She learns at last "no questions, no retorts : only silence." Unable to communicate her anxieties to the unapproachable, incommunicable, indifferent Mohan, she is overwhelmed and engulfed by a sense of seclusion. Eversince she gets married, she has done nothing but wait. "Waiting for Mohan to come home, waiting for the children to be born, for them to start school, waiting for them to come home, waiting for the milk, the servant, the lunch-carrier man" (Deshpande 1988 : 30). This mechanical process of waiting fills her life with the existential nothingness. Related to the theme of nothingness is the existential theme of death. At one point of the novel Jaya makes it clear : "And above the beyond this, there had been for me other waiting... waiting fearfully for disaster, for a catastrophe, I always had this feeling — that if I've escaped it today, it's still there round the corner waiting for me; the locked door, the empty house, the messenger of doom bringing news of death" (Deshpande 1988 : 30).

Jaya's sexual life gives her no satisfaction. She is not able to endure 'a silent, wordless lovemaking'. Sex with Mohan has become very mechanical. She says : "I could stay apart from him without a twinge, I could sleep with him, too, without desire" (Deshpande 1988 : 97). As one of Sartre's characters says, it is like drinking oneself without feeling thirsty (Sartre 1947 : 52). It is like the pointlessness experienced by T.S. Eliot's typist girl in 'The Waste Land'. To Jaya sex becomes, in the final count, extraneous. She also realises the fact that it is the act of sex that really affirms her loneliness. Mohan's indifference in and after sex often fills her with a sense of loneliness and of illusion : "But, lying there my body still warm and throbbing from the contact with his, it had come to me in one awful moment — that I was alone. The contact, the coming together, had been not only momentary, but wholly illusory as well. We had never come together, only our bodies had done that. I had begun to cry then, despairingly, silently, scared that I would wake Mohan up, trying desperately, to calm myself" (Deshpande 1988 : 98). One can notice here the dissolution of a feminine sensibility under the stress of marriage that finally destroys woman's being. This situation of Jaya reminds us to Maya's predicament in Anita Desai's *Cry, The Peacock*. Her husband is cold, hard and distant. She is lonely : "He did not give another thought to me, to either the soft, willing body or the lonely, wanting mind that waited near his bed" (Desai 1980 : 9).

On various occasions, Jaya is seen feeling a sense of nothingness and of mechanisation : "For us, there was just living — one foot in front of another, one foot in front of another, until death came to us in a natural form" (Deshpande 1988 : 4).

"It was not the conundrum of what we were to do with our lives that confronted us; it was a simple puzzle — what are we to do with ourselves this moment, this day, the next moment the next day..." (Deshpande 1988 : 24). These questions are similar to those of the neurotic woman seen in T.S. Eliot's "The Waste Land."

> "What shall I do now? What shall I do?
> ....
> .... what shall we do tomorrow?
> What shall we ever do?" (Eliot 1965 : 95).

This tells us the fact that Jaya is experiencing existential dilemma which is the outcome of human nothingness. She is living then without anything to structure her being and her world, and she is looking into emptiness and the void, hovering over the abyss in fear and trembling and living the life of dread. So she finds no answers for her questions : "But there was no answer to the question. It seemed to be flung into an abyss. Nothing returned, not even an echo..." (Deshpande 1988 : 24).

The particular situation of woman, Jaya understands, leads her not into anger. 'A woman can never be angry; she can only be neurotic, hysterical, frustrated" (Deshpande 1988 : 147). The reference made to the 'Woman sitting silently infront of the fire' and the incident where a woman silently weeps when her husband is beating her are meant for this revelation only. The death of Kusum is one more example for the nervy temperament of women. Jaya has also suffered silently when she stays alone in a seedy flat thinking of her husband who has gone away while an enquiry into his suspected malpractice is pursued and of the children who are away with a relative. In this curious situation, Jaya has undergone a real turmoil.

The kind of imagery the novelist makes use of is suitable to the existential themes of the novel. Jaya can compare wife and husband to "Two bullocks yoked together." The image of stationary train is used to convey something deeper in the sense that one's own movement in it is only our illusion. The conversation arranged between Jaya and Mukta about rebirth is also related to the main concerns of the novel :

'It used to seem meaningless to me — just one futile life after another, each one a cipher ending in nothing and the total, after so many births, again nothing. But now I feel it gives you a chance to redeem the failures of this life, doesn't it if you have another life?'

'But isn't being born again itself a failure? Isn't the real goal, the success, not to be born at all?' (Deshpande 88 : 184). The book is replete with existential watchwords such as 'absurdity', 'nothingness', 'emptiness', 'death', 'frustration', 'lonely', 'loneliness', 'anxiety' and 'silence'.

"The essence of modernism in the Indian English novel manifests itself most distinctly in the existentialistic trend" (Kalinnikova 1974 : 174). Shashi Deshpande's novels well exemplify this statement. *That Long Silence* is found to be more suitable to the existential trend. The experience of Jaya both as a woman and human being explains us this fact. The novel ends when Jaya comes to a conclusion that "life has always to be made possible." She almost reminds us here of Saru in Sashi Deshpande's *The Dark Holds No Terrors* (1980). All Saru wants is to "sleep peacefully the night through. To wake up without pain. To go through tomorrow without apprehension. Not to think, not to dream. Just to live" (Deshpande 1980 : 23). Jaya speaks not like a woman liberated from the burdens of either her humanity or her womanhood but a woman redefining her existential situation in her own terms, having it out 'on her own premises'. "Each self-aware individual understands his own existence in terms of his experience of himself and of his own situation" (Flew 1979 : 108).

Jaya's is not the voice of either metaphysical or social rebellion but of acceptance of the human condition and the predicament of her life as a woman. It is an acceptance with a difference, however, a declaration that, as a woman and as a writer, she is trying to cope. Because, existentialism is an attempt to reaffirm an individual's personal identity which is in danger of being eroded by deceptions, under the influence and demands of society. It also vindicates the individual despite his limitations and failures by insisting that he can transcend facticity in his own consciousness.

REFERENCES

Anita Desai, 1980, *Cry, The Peacock*, New Delhi : Orient paperbacks.

Shashi Desphande, 1980, *The Dark Holds No Terrors*, New Delhi : Vikas Publishing House.

—— 1988, *That Long Silence*, New Delhi : Penguin Books.

Eliot, T.S., 'The Waste Land', *The Faber Book of Modern Verse*, 91-104, London : Faber and Faber.

Flew, Antony, 1979, *A Dictionary of Philosophy*, London : Pan Book Ltd.

Kalinnikova, Elena J., 1982, *Indian-English Literature*, Gaziabad : Vimal Prakashan.

Lavine, T.Z., 1984, *From Socrates to Sartre : The Philosophic Quest*, New York : Bantam Books.

Morrison, Toni, 1987, *Beloved*, New York : Plume.

Sartre, Jean-Paul, 1947, *The Age of Reason*, Hamish Hamilton.

Walsh, William, 1990, *Indian Literature in English*, New York : Longman.

18

Rural Life Enmeshed in Traditional Ills : T.V. Reddy's *The Vultures*

P. BAYAPA REDDY

Among the recent Indian novelists in English T.V. Reddy has emerged as a potential creative artist reflecting the social milieu of the rural India at the end of the twentieth century. *The Vultures*,[1] his novel that came out from his powerful pen, has drawn appreciation from a noted contemporary novelist Dr. Narendrapal Singh who "recommends the novel to all those who want to understand India and its people."[2] When most of the novelists in Indian English indulge luxuriously in making excursions to distant and alien pastures, T.V. Reddy, with his extra-ordinary control over matter as well as medium, confines himself to the native soil and to the faithful presentation of his region. The distinction of the novelist lies in the fact that the vivisection of the society he presents, transcends the confines of the particular and embraces the universal.

With a spirit of restraint and artistic control, the novelist makes a faithful presentation of the rural life by recreating the spirit of feudalism that still rules the rural world. The uniqueness of this novel lies in the fact that it resists the temptation to sermonise which is not uncommon in Indo-Anglian fiction.

The Vultures comes before us as a true document of the rural life inseparable from the fields, farmers, bulls and cows. The activities of the villagers, both men and women, at home and in the fields, are vividly presented and their social life brought with the wealth of nature or blighted with economic misfortunes, is put forward graphically. The social background, the existing traditional setting, the ways of living of the villagers, their crisscross relationships and social contrasts are in as realistic a manner as possible. In other words, the novel is filled with the Indian sensibility. It is a true document of the social life, mostly rural life in India and nowhere does the writer make either a covert or over attempt to make any slight deviation from the rural setting nor does he bring any remote reference to the land outside India nor bring in the alien atmosphere.

The plot is woven round the life of a poor farmer Ramayya in a remote village of Siripalle in the Rayalaseema region of Andhra Pradesh, India. This simple and good-natured farmer and his wife Parvathi have a son and a daughter, Suresh and Santhi respectively. The father spends considerable amount on the collegiate education of his son for which he has raised loans from the rural bank and also from Rudraiah, the village head and money-lender. Rudraiah has a total monopoly of land, money and men and he along with Gangu, his muscle man, has complete control over the village. Naturally does his son Nagaraju become a spoiled child who with his depraved conduct, breaks all barriers in satiating his lust. The unemployment of the son worsens the economic plight of Ramayya. When he fails to clear off the loan, his bulls for which he has developed much sentimental attachment, are taken away by the bank people. Ramayya's daughter Santhi, commits suicide when she cannot protect her chastity from the landlord's son Nagaraju.

Her brother Suresh after knowing the truth at a later date, takes Nagaraju and Gangu to task. The beaten men wait like wolves for their opportunity and after a few days waylay Suresh on one dark and eerie night and stealthily hit him on the head with a stout stick. Suresh dies instantaneously. After a few days, Ramayya and Parvathi who are resigned to their lot, are seen returning home at sunset with their cow. The silence of the dark hours of the village is disturbed by Narayana's chanting of a famous hymn from the sacred book, Bhagavad Gita. This in brief, is the plot of the novel.

Set in a remote village, near the river Kalyani, *The Vultures* succeeds in its aim of re-creating rural life of the village atmosphere on a hot summer evening. Ramayya, a small farmer, in seen dragging his wearied feet homeward from his arid fields. With a plough on his shoulder, a whip in his hand, and a pair of bulls in front of him, he plods his way crossing a continuous stretch of barren land. "The weather is as still as death and the air is torpid; occasionally a gust of hot wind blew combining the earth and the sky with a thin film of dry dust blowing the same into the eyes of the people moving in the streets" (*The Vultures* p. 2). It is a typical Indian village consisting mostly of thatched houses and elevated stone platforms in front of the houses. Ramayya lives in a humble hut, rectangular in its shape with mud walls. A small kerosene lamp burns inside the hut. Outside the house, there is a semi permanent pandal resting stone pillar and the pandal is erected with tall horizontal bamboo sticks tightly tied with palmyra fibre above which is securely stacked.

Next is given a pictorial description of the busy activities of the village in the morning. The house wives rise early at dawn and start their day's work. They sweep in the open place in front of their houses and in the respective parts of the street, sprinkle dense water mixed with cowdung and decorate the ground with various floor designs. Men are seen busily and briskly walking to their fields driving their bullocks and controlling them separately by holding their ropes and carrying the yokes on their shoulders. Thus, the novel bristles with pictorial description of the rural scene.

The Vultures is a faithful record of all the unremitting hardships and problems, social as well as economic, encountered by the poor farmers and peasants. Ramayya is a poor farmer who educates his son by raising loans from the village head and also from the rural banks. At this juncture, he needs some more money for his son's education and when he goes to Rudraiah, the village head, for a small loan of two hundred rupees, the latter replies cunningly — 'With what face do you ask me money again? Nearly five years ago you took from me a loan of three thousand rupees which has now come to five thousand rupees with interest. You have paid me back neither principal nor interest' (pp. 25-26). When the poor farmer requests him again saying that he is ready to abide by his terms, the moneylender in his characteristic way replies : 'I shall help you by giving the loan provided you mortgage your hut along with the site'. Ramayya in his helpless situation, bows to his callous conditions. Through such common place situations the novelist highlights the world of exploitation by the power of money.

What is remarkable in this novel is that it mirrors not only the exploitation of the poor by the rich, but also the exploitation of the poor by the poor and by the bureaucrats. While Ramayya wants to till the land by arranging a few ploughs, the ploughman Polayya doesn't turn up on the day of ploughing as he goes away for the landlord Rudraiah. Another coolie goes very late to work. Ramayya feels very much pained and he expresses his anger by saying that though he gives higher wages than the Sarpanch gives, the peasants do not keep their word. While the coolies go early to the rich man to work in the field and take less wages from him, they come late to work for the poor farmers and take higher wages from them. This is an instance of the writer's close observation of the exploitation of the poor by the poor which is always a common feature in the villages.

The novel unfolds effectively the cruelties of the landlords and the corrupt practices of the bureaucrats who appear as mild creatures before political leaders, but become wild before the poor. The personnel of the rural bank bring an official order for the attachment of the defaulter's property and they attempt to throw away the vessels from Ramayya's thatched house. The officer, drunk with power and pride, shouts angrily at the poor farmer — 'You think the loan amount is your grand father's property. Either you pay or we have to auction' (p. 36). Though the awkward situation is averted for the present through the intervention of the Sarpanch, the rural bank officer's corrupt nature is exposed when on his instruction, his peon takes 'Mamul' (a bribe) from the poor farmer. After the storm is ever, the helpless farmer, recollects that he got a loan of Rs. 500/- from the co-operative bank by supplying to the co-operative supervisor a cartload of firewood.

The novelist's observation of men and matters in the society is so close and chillingly realistic that even the trivial incident of bribing petty forest officials for getting a cartload of firewood doesn't miss his powerful eye. Later when the officials seize Ramayya's two bulls — Bhima and Basava — for the non-clearance of the loan, the farmer is grief-stricken and he feels as though his own children are snatched away. Losing his characteristic self-restraint, Suresh shouts sardonically — 'You are not Government servants; your are devil's servants' (p. 133).

The novel presents a ghastly picture of the social evil of dowry. Ramayya, being economically hard-pressed, finds it beyond his means to perform the marriage of his only daughter Santhi. Being too poor to 'buy' the bridegroom with heavy dowry, he goes on postponing the crisis of finding a suitable alliance for his good looking daughter. When he feels happy at the proposal of Gopal as an eligible match, suddenly he meets with disappointment as well as distress when Srinivas, the boy's father, demands both money and gold besides the huge expenditure to be incurred by the girl's father in celebrating the marriage. The clever statement of Srinivas — 'For my part I do not like to take dowry. But one who does not take dowry is looked down upon' (p. 89) — reveals his sinister motives. At the deeper level, it reveals to us the cancerous evil of dowry that is consuming the body and soul of society. Had Santhi's marriage with Gopal been materialized, her sorrowful end would not have taken place. In a sense, the monstrous devil of dowry system is responsible for Santhi's untimely death. The novelist succeeds in presenting the existing social evils and from many angles this novel is a great achievement as it presents the social ills and problems through situations in an entirely realistic manner without ever making any overt attempt to moralize or sermonize or philosophize.

The social consciousness of the writer is discernible in the title itself. The title is only too apt literally as well as metaphorically for Rudraiah, his son and his servant are the worst vultures. While Rudraiah is a cruel extortioner, his son is a drunkard and rapist ruining the lives of young girls of poor and working classes. His servant Gangu is a follower of his unscrupulous master. He is illiterate and ignorant, wicked and beastly. While Rudraiah is never tired of indulging in the clever game of amassing wealth by crooked ways, his lieutenant Gangu supports blindly his wicked master and the master's son. He is a typical village head who gives loans to the poor farmers only when they mortgage their houses or lands which finally go to him as most of them cannot get them released. The inhuman nature of Rudraiah is revealed when he gives clandestine instructions to his "musclemen" to burn Ramayya's hay-stack. As the poor farmer is already deprived of his bulls, he looks at the heap of ashes of his hay with stoic resignation. This dastardly act pierces his wife's gentle heart. Even a proud and powerful Rudraiah cannot escape the sting of irony when he is covertly cheated by his trusted servant Gangu, who establishes an illegal sexual relation with his wife. When the master goes to the city seeking fresh pastures of pleasures, the servant makes use of his absence by making a free play of illicit sex with the sexually starved wife of his master.

In a family of vices, Sandhya is the only exception, being a sensitive and scrupulous young lady. Her brother Nagaraju grows to be an irresponsible rake under the protective wings of his father. He spreads the ripples of hysteria in the placid village; still no one has the courage to curb him. Who ever is fair among the working class women, falls a prey to his lust; first Leela is about to fall a victim and then Santhi has in fact fallen a prey. When the truth of his foul deed suddenly reaches Suresh, he attacks him in great fury, beats his supporter too fiercely resulting in his pitiable death on one stormy night. The presentation of the situation is so realistic that the reader is not permitted to miss the observance of the truth of the natural subsiding of the case of an unnatural death of the young man. It is an indication of the fact that justice is afraid of even winking at the injustice done to the poor and the weak and closes her eyelids to the foul acts and dark deeds of the rich and the powerful.

The novelist with his practical observation of the rural life, lashes out at the Panchayat Raj system. His incidental remarks on the system of Panchayat Raj reveal the dangers and the negative aspects of the system — 'Ever since the Panchayat Raj came into existence with its elections, even an erstwhile peaceful village in a remote corner of the country is torn asunder in political factions and petty feuds and the modern Indian village has become a cockpit of quarrels, hatred, jealousies, rivalries and riots' (p. 139). The novelist, whose prime interest is the well-being of the village and the welfare of the society, after carefully analysing the rural situation, boldly makes his clinical assessment. The traditional opinion regarding the calm, quiet and happy atmosphere of the village life is exploded by this rural-based writer.

It is quite interesting to see that the novelist does not spare even the present system of education which is being experimented time and again by the Government. He feels that the system of education of the yester years was quality-based and it aimed at depth and durability of learning while the modern system aims at width and breadth of knowledge and is made a diseased patient and kept always on the operation table by the government and the educationists. What is implicitly spelt out is the fact that 'Veethi-badi' or 'the school under the greenwood tree in the street' is better than the modern school equipped with audio-video facilities.

Thus, the novelist within the limited compass of the novel, has succeeded in projecting the rural life enmeshed by sociological, political and economic problems and other traditional ills. In the words of D.C. Chambial "Like Charles Dickens, Mr. Reddy is all set to hold a mirror to the society full of money and pitfalls for the poor, honest and god-fearing men and women."[3] It would be quite interesting to compare this novel with Kamala Markandaya's *Nectar in a Sieve.* Though both the novels deal with the peasant life and rural setting, *The Vultures* re-creates the Indian atmosphere as well as Indian sensibility, while *Nectar in a Sieve* presents the Indian as well as alien background and doesn't succeed in presenting Indian sensibility in a credible manner. While Ramayya and Parvathi, even after their terrible loss of their children and the pair of bulls, continue to live in their village with philosophical resignation and resume their toiling and moiling in an inherently dignified manner, Rukmani and Nathan in *Nectar in a Sieve*, in a more or less similar situation, leave the village, go to a remote town in search of their working son, lose their heart and strength in conviction, and reduce themselves to the degraded level of beggars fighting for alms in the form of 'Prasadam' at the temple. Thus, the novelist is seen as a keen observer of our society in delineating the tragic drama of the poor rural folk, who constitute the vast majority of Indian population. Reddy's *The Vultures* is one of the best fictional chronicles of our time based on reality.

REFERENCES

1. T.V. Reddy, *The Vultures*, Calcutta : Golden Books, 1983. All the textual references are from this edition only.
2. Review by Dr. Narendrapal Singh, *By Word*, New Delhi, October 1985, p. 50.
3. Review by D.C. Chambial *Bharat Protiva*, Calcutta, September-October, 1984

19

Triumph of Desire over Renunciation : Gita Mehta's *A River Sutra*

PARASURAM RAMAMOORTHI

"It is the story of Man" — the celebrated Peter Brook Version of the Mahabharata declared and we have innumerable instances of commentators speaking of the Epic as the tale of human suffering and the triumph of Good over Evil. It is not an accident that the Novel is set on the banks of river Narmada, a deliberate attempt to link it with *The Mahabharata* which was first dictated by sage Vyasa on the banks of river Narmada, thousands of years ago. If The Mahabharata is a story of the battle between Dharm and Adharm and the final victory of Dharm *A River Sutra* is the story of the battle between Desire and Renunciation and the triumph of Desire over Renunciation. It is also the war between Instinct and Reason and the Instinct triumphs.

The Novel is a celebration of Life and life-affirming impulses struggling against Death and life-negating forces. The River is seen as an eternal principle of Life. The Naga Baba who became an ascetic and lived in a cave seeking higher enlightenment "reentered the world" (p. 282) with the knowledge that "I am only a man." He tells the Narrator "Don't you know the soul must travel through eighty-four thousand births in order to become a man." The epigraph to the novel, a song from Chandidas also points to the central principle of celebration of Man :

> Listen, O brother
> Man is the greatest truth.
> Nothing beyond.

If Man is the greatest Truth, how can one seek the Truth

running away from mankind. All attempts to renounce the world come to nothing and they become temporary escapes from the Reality. C.N. Ramachandran commenting on the various tales in the Novel asserts that "what we get at the end of the novel is a multiple vision of the 'many-coloured dome' — Life" (Gita Mehta's — *A River Sutra* : Two views "*The Literary Criterion* Vol. 29, No. 3. 1994, p. 5). Prof. Ramachandran also speaks of the contrapuntal pulls between attachment and detachment and he affirms that the novel "rejects the concept of total detachment as well".

The Bureaucrat — Narrator keeps asking questions about life to the people he meets. He tries to understand Life through questioning. He is willing to listen to the stories of others and through the stories reason out the meaning of Life. In the first inset story of the Jain Monk, towards the end, The Monk grows tired of his questions and tells him : No, I cannot stay longer. You must find someone else to answer your questions (p. 41). He tells the Monk that he also has renounced the world and has the humility to ask the Monk the reason for his renunciation and what was the most difficult thing to give up. He asks the Monk to enlighten him with his story and he is willing to sit by his side and listen to the Monk's story. But at the end of the story the Narrator simply feels disturbed and the lasting impact is that the image of the Monk is imprinted in his mind.

When we analyse the stories of the Narrator and the Monk, it becomes evident that the Narrator retires from active life hoping to find the meaning of Life and it is like a planned Vanaprasthi. It almost looks like that one would say I have worked for so many years in cities. "I have nobody. My wife is dead. So, I should go into the forest for Vanaprasthi." He does not renounce his job. But prefers a less important job in a remote place on the banks of Narmada. There is so much planning and hardwork that point to his reasoning. The Monk, suddenly, decides to give up wealth, wife, children, friends, and all the comforts of a luxurious living. His decision is based on intuition and faith whereas the Narrator's life is one pursuit guided by reason. The Narrator's friend Tariq Mia explains what the Monk's story means : The human heart has only one secret. The capacity to love (p. 48). This secret is beyond the comprehension of Reason.

Tariq Mia's narration of the story of Music Teacher, Master Mohan is meant to prick the pride of the Narrator : Drink some tea, little brother. How can you say you have given up the world when you know so little of it?, says, Tariq Mia and begins the story of Master Mohan, a Story meant to understand "the ways of the human heart" (p. 50).

Master Mohan, by chance, found a boy and groomed him in Music and later discovered that the boy to be a prodigy. The boy's singing became so popular that a great Sahib invited him to sing at his place. But Master Mohan refused. Master Mohan's wife who wanted to make some money out of the boy accepted the offer and received five thousand rupees. Later the boy was forced to sing and he sang such notes that it filled the hall with ecstasy and mystic raptures. Suddenly the Great Sahib rose and Master Mohan thought that the Sahib, like the Sufis, was going to dance to the Music of the Boy, but realized, only after it happened, that the Sahib slit the throat of the boy and his logic was cold and cruel : such a voice is not human. What will happen to music if this is the standard by which God judges us? (p. 89). This story leaves the narrator with many questions unanswered. From simple questions like, "But did the police catch the great sahib?" to why did the Sahib kill the boy. Tariq Mia's explanation is that "I don't know the answer, little brother. It is only a story about the human heart" (p. 91).

The Executive's story is also built on instinct. He falls in love with a Coolie's wife after making love to her in darkness for several nights. When he returns to the city and gets lost in the glitter of society-ladies, he still is haunted by the love song of that tribal woman, Rima. Nitin Bose, the executive visits the tea estate again, he encounters Rima and is subjected to some kind of tribal magic. It is believed that he is possessed and he believes that he is a woman. The tribal priest tells Nitin Bose that only the River has been given the power to cure and so he is taken to the river bed where he will immerse the figure of a goddess. The narrator and his assistant watch the scene from a secret place. When the narrator finished reading Nitin Bose's story it made no sense to him. But his assistant Chagla understands it intuitively and explains : The goddess is just the principle of life. She is every illusion that is inspiring love (p. 142). Chagla goes on to explain that "without desire, there is no life. Everything will stand still. Become emptiness. In fact sir, be dead" (p. 142).

The story of the Courtezan, narrated by her mother and herself, is a tale of belief and faith based on intuition. Rahul Singh the notorious bandit kidnaps the young courtezan and keeps her in captivity in a cave. She refuses to surrender to him sexually and when he tells her that she had been his wife in many births before this one, she refuses to believe him. But, one night when he touched her, she realized that she had been his wife in many lives before : Guided by his touch, I learned I had known his body in a hundred lifetimes before he took me again a virgin on the thin quilt which was all that shielded our bodies from the ground (p. 184). Her mysterious disappearance near the cliffs and the mother reporting that her daughter is dead are full of improbabilities. "Nonsense, Chagla. The daughter was here, in my office, only half an hour ago" (p. 189) — the narrator expresses his disbelief. On the whole the story seems like a tall-tale for a man of reason. The reader does not question like the narrator, having known the narrator through many such stories.

The story of the Musician who loved Music and his daughter again leaves the narrator with suspicion. When the girl tells him that she learnt Music alongwith another young man from her father on the condition that the young man will marry her and how finally the man got married to someone else, she was left desolate. Her father told her to meditate on the waters of the Narmada until she is cured of her attachment to her lover so that she can become again the ragini to every raga. She must become the bride of Music. The narrator looks at Tariq Mia in disbelief and questions : Of course not. The beauty of the Narmada makes it a perfect retreat for anyone like myself wishing to withdraw from the world. But how can it exorcise a lover's grief? (p. 227).

A River Sutra ends again in a note of not being sure of anything. The narrator cannot believe that Dr. Shankar was once an ascetic and now a mere admirer of Narmada. "I stood there in the darkness watching them, unable to believe he had ever been a naked ascetic, unable to convince myself he had not" (p. 282).

A River Sutra is essentially a novel about river Narmada and the novel gains much of its significance and meaning with the river as the central character. We have instances of a river being a major character in Mark Twain's *Adventures of Huckleberry Finn* and in several regional novels in India. Laksmi's *Kaveriai Pola* is an excellent example from Tamil Fiction where the river comes to be identified with the central character, a woman. A.K. Ramanujam's "A River" and R. Parthasarathy's Poem on Vaigai and many other poems also speak of the modern perspectives on ancient rivers. But *A River Sutra* is quite different from all these works of literature, in that it focuses on the riverbased civilisation and its beliefs. *A River Sutra* is a record of the human race as it depicts the struggle between the Pre-Aryan life and the Aryan conquest. The Pre-Aryans managed to fight against the Aryans, but eventually lost the battle and the only source of comfort to them is Narmada and the banks of Narmada are their refuge. They worship the River and believe that the river has the power to cure many diseases, including madness and snake venom.

The river Narmada is described in many ways : it is the holiest pilgrimage site (p. 3), daughter of God Shiva (p. 3), it is a link between mankind and the energy of Shiva (p. 8), and married to the ocean, Lord of Rivers (p. 9). It is the site of Vyasa's recitation of *The Mahabharata*, Kabir's poems, Kalidasa's *Meghdoot*. The Novel is a myth of the river and the novelist has succeeded in the myth-making.

River Narmada is the daughter of Shiva. The novelist turns a geographical reality into a myth and her myth-making is part of the Indian Psyche which turns every fact of the creation of the universe into a myth.

> It is said that Shiva, Creator and Destroyer of worlds, was in an ascetic trance so strenuous that rivulets of perspiration began flowing from his body down the hills. The stream took on the form of a woman — the most dangerous of her kind : a beautiful virgin innocently tempting even ascetics to pursue her, inflaming their lust by appearing at one moment as a lightly dancing girl, at another as a romantic dreamer, at yet another as a seductress loose-limbed with the lassitude of desire. Her inventive variations so amused Shiva that he named her Narmada, the Delightful One, blessing her with the words "You shall be forever holy, forever inexhaustible" (pp. 8-9).

The river appears as a woman "indolently stretching her limbs as she oiled herself with scented oils," as a woman "painting her palms and the soles of her feet with vermilion as she prepared to meet her lover" (p. 139). On the banks of the river, mystic rituals are enacted by Vano villagers, the remnants of Pre-Aryan Civilisation. The tribals will pray to their goddess to forgive anyone who has denied the power of desire. Even Lord Shiva could not deny the power of Desire, because without desire there is no life. The Pre-Aryan Goddess is the "principle of life. She is every illusion that is inspiring love." When pilgrims chant "Save us from the serpent's venom", the serpent is nothing but desire.

Contraries is the principle of life. In most of us, there are two tendencies : to create fantasy and to kill that fantasy. We are increasingly lured by our scientific and rational thinking to kill the fantasy. We laugh at experiences like trance and being possessed. Dr. Mitra, the doctor who attended on Nitin Bose, the executive, has his own contribution to the many legends about Narmada. He says that the war between the "primal beliefs of the tribals and Aryan reason" was fought on the banks of the river. He recalls the meaning of "Narmada" as "Whore". He is a scholar on the river Narmada. He tells the narrator :

> Her holiness is believed to dispel the malevolent effects of Saturn, so all manner of epileptics, depressives, and other unfortunates rush to her banks. And yet, the Narmada is also a magnet to scholars (p. 153).

Dr. Mitra's attraction towards the river has its own story and he is full of information about the river. He says that "even the war between the Aryans and the pre-Aryans is still unresolved here" (p. 153) and he informs that four thousand year old Aryan warrior still lives on the north bank of Narmada and his name is Avatihuma. Several songs about the glory of Narmada are sung by river minstrels :

> You leap through the earth
> Like a dancing deer.
> The devout call you Rewa
> The leaping one (p. 273).

The sages meditating on your river banks say :

> You are twice-born,

Once from penance,
Once from love (p. 275).

Such songs record human sentiments and fears about the river. Though Dr. Shankar brushes aside all these legends, he accepts the fact "If anything is sacred about the river, it is the individual experiences of the human beings who have lived here" (p. 264). The river is a source of information for Dr. Shankar who believes that there is evidence of human life during the Stone Age in one of the caves near the river. Dr. Shankar also dismisses the idea that the river can be a place for Vanaprasthi, because "too many lives converge on these banks" (p. 268).

You were present at the Creation
By Shiva's command you alone will remain
At the Destruction (p. 277).

All these stories converge at one point, that the river is a perennial source of Life and hence immortal. The river has witnessed the passing of civilisations and the songs celebrate her immortality. The beliefs about the powers of the river are manifestations of Man's faith in the River Narmada as against the rational mind's curiosity to know about Human Race.

A River Sutra can easily be described as "Metaphysical Novel." Edwin M. Eigner in his book *The Metaphysical Novel in England and America* published in 1978 (Berkley : University of California Press) defined the novel as one which "often infests itself in a dim and shadowy allegory" (p. 6) and the novel follows its own drift, set in "suitable remoteness", with a passive hero. Characters undertake chartless voyages against the tyranny of everyday life. The structure of a Metaphysical Novel is determined by multiple voiced narration and the mixture of genres. It employs a realistic beginning and grows in the direction of Allegory and the end purpose is to arrive at the redeeming vision for Man. It is a breakaway from the cause and-effect world (pp. 7-12)

The above definition well fits *A River Sutra* with its multiple narrative strategies and a passive hero as the central character. The principal narrator, a bureaucrat on the verge of retirement, attempts to tell his story, but he is told several stories by others. The framing is that of the Bureaucrat's story and there are inset in the frame stories of the Monk, Executive, Courtezan, Teacher, Minstrel and within these stories, there are stories of Shiva, Narmada, Kabirvad, Avatihuma, and hundreds of legends inlaid within the frame. The narrative flows like the river and the endless voyage of human beings over the ages. There is not much of a pause between one story and the other. It easily switches over from one story to another. The only difficulty with these stories is that almost all of them use the same dialect and the language does not change with the narrator. The principal narrator tells a story and he is being told stories. The narrator becomes a listener or the reader. The contract between Gita Mehta and the readers is symbiotic of the relationship between the Bureaucrat and the various story-tellers. He is amused, amazed, shocked, surprised, disturbed, and what is significant is the fact that he is in the same state of confusion even at the end of the novel. There is no self-realization, no epiphany and not even a Frostian wisdom achieved.

Gita Mehta presents the principal narrator as a fugitive and some of the characters in the stories resemble him. A.G. Khan in an interesting article (The Literary Criterion, Vol. 29, No. 3. 1994, pp. 7-15) identifies him with the Monk, Master Mohan, Executive, Naga Baba and Mr. Shankar and comments that all these characters try to escape from everyday reality, wealth, luxury, money, woman and go in search of peace, Nirvana, Freedom and enlightenment. Most of them do not see light at the end of the tunnel and characters like Tariq Mia do not run away from the reality and comprehend what they think is the meaning of life. To some, desire is the principle of life and to some to love humanity is the meaning of life. *A River Sutra* in this angle may be an allegory of Life itself and the various sutras are like the fabrics of Life.

The novel set in a remote forest on the banks of Narmada meanders through Assam with the valleys of Vindhya, the plains of Malva and metaphysically set in two different banks of the river where the river separates the beliefs and calendars and histories. Pre-Aryan and Aryan settings are imaged through the novel and essentially the novel is an attempt at a flight from Realism. The remoteness is of the mind, though set in a never-land or a land of the mind; a kind of Mindscape is painted. The obvious difference between the outer world and the Mindscape is brought into limelight so that we journey through the Mindscape without trembling the falling into some ditch.

Against the backdrop of Narmada Bachao Andolan and Medha Patkar's activities, a scene from contemporary socio-political scene, Gita Mehta's *A River Sutra* is an attempt at subversiveness to present the river as an eternal source of the flow of Life.

> Turtles and river dolphins find refuge in your waters
> Alighting herons play upon your tranquil surface.
> Fish and crocodiles are gathered in your embrace.
> O holy Narmada.
> Bards and ascetics sing your wonders.
> Gamblers, cheats, and dancers praise you.
> We all find refuge in your embrace, O holy Narmada
> (p. 279).

●

PART B

20

A Synthesis of Socialist and Structuralist Perspectives : Chinappa Bharati's *Sangam*

K. CHELLAPPAN

'A rare great epic — the life of people living in the hilly region' says Kannan, in his Foreward to *Sangam* (1985) of Chinappa Bharati. He also says that in this novel, history blooms as story and it is a triumph of socialist realism as it probes into the story of exploitation in a realistic manner and unravels the economic forces that determine their lives and shows the need for the solidarity of the dispossessed to fight the evils. While we accept the presence of socialist realism in the novel, we would like to point out that its portrayal of the life of those people is close to Levi Strauss's structuralist analysis of the lives of the primitive tribes, though it is subordinated to the socialist perspective.

Marx and Engels make a reference to the link between man and nature and how man gets alienated from his true nature as well as his fellowmen when he gets estranged from nature. According to Marx :

> The human significance of nature only exists for social man, because only in this case is nature a bond with other men. Only then is nature the basis of his own human experience and a vital element of human reality. The natural existence of man has here become his human existence and nature itself has become human for him.

> Thus, society is the accomplished union of man with nature, the veritable resurrection of nature, the realised naturalism of man and the realised humanism of nature.[1]

The hill people are very close to nature and right in the beginning, the novel gives a picture of man living in harmony with nature. The music of the bells around the neck of the bulls mingles with the spotless melody of the cuckoo; the organ music of the sparrow and others finally links with the music of waters flowing melodiously. Then, the hill tops, then small hills and finally the plains with the groves full of variety of fruit trees.

Significantly, the description ends with two thorny bushes in the dry land. The next para contrasts this natural environment with the heap of dust and the smoke in the city and describes it as the natural environment with a virginity unravished by the artificial onslaughts of the machine age — such is the nature of the people too.

This Edenic harmony is disturbed by the intrusion of a jeep which came jolting like a strange fairy (goddess). The simile is significant as it signifies the invasion of alien values with a mysterious look. This is the beginning of problems for Tiruman, the protagonist of the novel as it brought an officer and an intermediary who simply forced him to give as penalty a lot of fruits etc. for no fault of his. The author then portrays the way in which men and women worked in the field, singing songs together and sharing their food. Their life was characterised by ceaseless hardwork, by both men and women, though they are distinguished by the two kinds of work they did.

On the one hand, man has to work hard in conflict with nature to quench the flame of the hunger. On the other, the field was glittering like a virgin girl — here again, there is the humanisation of nature. And their song comes as an antidote to their struggles and work.

Besides fulfilling their basic needs, the people in this part had to think of prestige of the family. There is a subtle link between their attachment to the pigs (nature) and the money value which is linked to their daughter's marriage. Whereas, there is a subtle link between man and nature, as the hill protects those who live in harmony with it, the market signifies exploitation of man by man because of the dominance of commercial values which bring deceit. Whereas Tiruman becomes a victim to the exploiting order and is thinking of selling the pigs to buy clothes for his daughter, his son has a practical approach. Tiruman's plight is caused because he is in the grip of age old traditions. According to his father, man must have a sacred relationship with the soil. But he is exploited because of the changing social relations and he is asked to pay penalty for having violated one such rule. But more than that was the loss of prestige.

> They could silently digest the evils, injustice and distress in their life struggle. But the insults and ignominies caused by the traditional dogmas will not allow them any peace of mind easily (p. 69).

In such a society, there are also other factors which contribute to a false consciousness or ideology (in Althusser's terms) which forces them to accept all injustices. The idea of God helps him to accept even the exploitation as something inevitable. Here is a projection of their social classifications upon the cosmic order as they think that some of the exploiters are instruments of God.

Even though the people do not give importance to the concepts such as chastity, they have certain norms. They feel that there is a link between violating such norms and their suffering. For *e.g.*, Ponnamal's difficulty in delivering the child.

There are also superstitions regarding the drying up of land and the need to appease the gods. Superimposed, upon it is the man-made convention of the person who demands women in exchange for the money *e.g.,* Sukran's taking away Vellayan's wife.

But there is also the other pull — a love for life and hope in Tiruman. He is basically good and that is why he is unable to give false evidence in the court on behalf of Tharmakartha (trustee) and he is happy to come back to the hill. But the need for changing the system is more explicit in Satayan, his son and his daughter. The hills to some extent signify "nature" — because still it has not gone beyond sexual cohabitation into the institution of marriage. According to Levi Strauss, to explain society is to explain how reciprocal exchanges come to exist — exchange of information, of goods, of power, rights and obligation and exogamy which is the basis of exchange — in the formation of society.

In this novel, Tiruman's daughter's desire to live a proper wedded life with one man and her parents' desire to achieve this symbolise a further stage of development from the natural into the social. Strangely, woman symbolising nature is also an agent of culture. According to Levi Strauss, there is a homology between nature/culture, female/male, such that female is nature and male culture. But, in certain cultures woman transforms men from a state of nature into social beings. Since women perform this through sexuality, sexuality itself can be called a natural social fact. But only when this sexuality is channelised through exchange, there is the economic and the symbolic over the biological and the natural. But in Tiruman, there is the combination of traditional and economic values — there is an element of economic exchange even when they fix the marriage, but still it is also linked with the soil. Sukran's act shows the dominance of the commercial over the cultural and biological and the act signifies degradation of woman into mere commodity.

When Vellayan tries to transcend this by going to the police as advised by Seerankan, he is almost crushed by the system because 'money' has corrupted even the judge. Then the need to organise a *Sangam* is felt by people like Satayan and this is made possible because Veluchamy is able to 'recover' Vellayan's wife from 'Kanthukaran'. Even Satayan questions the need to sign the bond and eventhough he is put in jail, there he is educated on the evils that afflict the hill people because of the exploitative system as well as their ideology. Satayan and a few others realise that if the exploited people raise their voices together and understand their problems in a realistic way, a new order will dawn. In this process, they are also supported by Ponnammal and Karumayi. Now, the only solution seems to have the market in their own place — on the hill and struggle to achieve this goal.

Satayan's own father is against all this because he has succumbed to an ideology which perpetuates evil. He is most upset and angry with his son when his grove is destroyed by the enemies of Satayan. But when there is an attempt to take away their land and destroy plants, Tiruman raises not only his voice but an axe to defend the soil which has been nourishing him and which he has nourished with his sweat and blood. This courage has come because he has experienced the onslaught of the evil forces. What a few acquire through study and lectures, he acquired in a minute through experiential reality. Though he is arrested, his son and others stand together for their land. When the other force withdraws, they shout triumphantly. "This land belongs to us Sangam will triumph. People will stay for ever." The first time the voice of earth, the warm breath of moral indignation, the sound of music coming from the power of the soul, the lofty determination of the declaration of freedom sprang up and reverberated in the hills like the roaring thunder (p. 332).

In conclusion, the novel tries to combine in its social analysis Levi Strauss's structuralism with socialism as it relates the happy life of the hill people to their closeness to nature but at the same time it shows its inner contradictions when it speaks of the crippling conventions both 'natural' and man-made. There in a link between the economic relations and their sexual life. Whereas the primitive has certain norms the exploiters use them for their own purpose and women become simply commodities. Opposed to this emerge the new economic/political awareness of Satayan and the cultural awareness of his sister.

The role of women in this society is rather ambiguous — they seem to be close to culture whereas men seem to be close to nature. But the real fact is that they are exploited and they stand for both nature and culture. While they accept their biological duties and marriage is more central to them, they convert biology into culture. Similarly, they also oppose the tyranny of the market world. The real solution is in understanding the real forces in the society and see them not as given and eternally immutable, but man-made and therefore they can be changed. So, both the progressive men and women do not accept the false theories attributed to nature and they want not only to *understand* and *interpret* life, but *change* it. It is here socialism comes in. But even then the novel does not simply show the triumph of culture over nature, because Tiruman's final protest comes out of his love for nature-his land, though here again there is culture, because it is not simply love for land — but *belonging* to it, as well as its *belonging* to him. That is why in the final analysis nature-culture dichotomy has only methodological and not ontological validity as both Derrida and Levi Strauss show it. Whereas Levi Strauss says :

> Above all, it is beginning to emerge that the distinction between nature and culture, while of no acceptable historical significance, does contain a logic, fully justifying its use by modern sociology as a methodological tool.

Derrida says :

> For, from the moment that the incest-prohibition can no longer be conceived within the nature/ culture opposition, it can no longer be said that it is a scandalous fact, a nucleus of opacity within a network of transparent significations. The incest-prohibition is no longer a scandal one meets with or comes up against in the domain of traditional concepts; it is something which escapes these concepts and certainly precedes them — probably as the condition of their possibility. It could perhaps be said that the whole of philosophical conceptualization, systematically relating itself to the nature/culture opposition, is designed to leave in the domain of the unthinkable the very thing that makes this conceptualization possible : the origin of the prohibition of incest.[2]

But if Derrida only shows the endlessness of free play of meanings which could lead to some radicalism Marx alone shows how an economic interpretation of society can lead to changing the society. And in *Sangam* we find an artistic rendering of such an interpretation of society, though linked with Levi Strauss's structuralist approach.

REFERENCES

1. Karl Marx, *Economic and Philosophical manuscripts* : Erick in *Mark's concept of Man*, New York, 1961, translated by T.B. Bottomore, pp. 131-2, 135.
2. Jacques Derrida, "Structure, Sign and Play in the discourse of the Human Sciences" Robert Con David & Ronald Schleifer (Ed.) *Contemporary Literary Criticism*, Longman : 1989, p: 317.

21

A Gandhian Novel with a Difference : Rajam Krishnan's *Verukku Nir*

P. MARUDANAYAGAM

Rajam Krishnan, a reputed woman novelist in her late sixties, has written many Tamil novels which are authentic and powerful expressions of Indian life in various parts of the country. She never writes about a community before she gains a first-hand knowledge of it by observing its life at close quarters. Her novels are vigorous pleas for the immediate uplift of the oppressed as well as for the promotion of the feminist cause. *Verukku Nir* (Water for the Roots), covering the events reported to have taken place in 1969, is a Gandhian novel with a difference. It is a far cry from Raja Rao's *Kanthapura*, hailed as a "Veritable grammar of the Gandhian myth."[1]

During the Gandhian age, far-reaching changes took place in almost every area of Indian life. In the words of Nehru, "Gandhi... was like a powerful current of fresh air that made us stretch ourselves and take deep breaths."[2] The unprecedented mass-awakening caused by the Gandhian whirlwind generated a national consciousness. His ideas on political, social, economic, cultural and spiritual issues — especially, his doctrines of soul-force, passive resistance, non-violence and purity of means, his insistence on women's freedom, condemnation of child marriage, the dowry system and enforced widowhood, his opposition to birth-control by artificial means and advocacy of self-control and voluntary chastity, his criticism of the evil of drinking, his plea for free, compulsory and self-supporting education through the mother tongue, his rejection of the concept of the economic man and refusal to divorce economics from ethics, his recommendation of the establishment of small, well-knit rural communities, his preachings of sarvodaya, swadeshi and khadi spinning and his stress on the need for voluntary acceptance of the ideas of trusteeship by the capitalists — provided the Indian writers writing in English or in any of their own languages with a number of profound themes. Using the Gandhian material, fiction flourished in our regional languages as well as in English. The impress of Gandhism was strong on the novels of K.S. Venkataramani. K. Nagarajan, Mulk Raj Anand, Raja Rao and on many more of the Gandhian era.

Kanthapura, the most splendid evocation of the Gandhian age, presents Gandhiji as the pride of the nation and gloats over the triumphant discovery of the Indian soul. The narrator of *Kanthapura* is an old brahmin widow, "largely a creature of memory and tradition, and herself a character in the action, though a strictly minor one; her intellectual range is limited, though she can agreeably respond to new ideas and situations".[3] Rajam Krishnan's Tamil novel written in the post-colonial period appropriately chooses a young female intellectual as its protagonist and point of view character. There is no attempt on the part of the author to distance herself from the heroine where the attitude to Gandhian philosophy and the message of the novel are concerned. All the experiences of the chief character may not be those of the novelist but there is no tinge of undercutting irony in the portrayal of the former.

The people living in the village called *Kanthapura*, very much like the masses of Gandhiji's time, firmly believe that he can do no wrong, can be guilty of no miscalculation. "They say that the Mahatma will go to the Red-man's country, and he will get us Swaraj... And we shall be happy."[4] But to one's horror, one witnesses an altogether different Indian city in *Verukku Nir*. Gandhiji is dead and gone; his principles are more remembered in their breach than in their observance; his true disciples are conspicuous by their absence.

One recalls that when Gandhiji was at the height of his fame C.F. Andrews expressed the hope that Gandhiji's name "will be remembered and sung by the village people long after the names of the modern governors in their palaces in New Delhi are forgotten."[5] But, unfortunately, even when the struggle for independence was coming to an end and freedom was in sight there was a maddened and unseemly rush for fishes and loaves of office. By the time the country marched into the sixties and seventies, a vast majority had learnt to exploit their name.

Verukku Nir is a history of our own times as well as a family chronicle, fusing in itself the personal and family perspectives and national concerns. The scene shifts from Ooty to Madras to Calcutta and to Patna running the entire gamut of Indian politics. Rajam Krishnan's preference for the mother-tongue as the medium and her stress on simplicity and clarity and her rejection of ornateness and conscious artistry reveal the Gandhian influence as much as her choice of themes and characters.

Verukku Nir presents a world in which :

> "The most dishonest, the most disreputable, the most corrupt politicians capitalize on his name, and everyday he is being assassinated, not in the body but in the spirit."[6]

Evoking the atmosphere of the novel, the opening chapters describe the Gandhi birth centenary celebrations at Geetha Mahal in Ooty organized by a Sevashram in order to highlight Gandhiji's message of love and ahimsa. The programme, in which most participants are young ashram children of the *Irular* community of the area, has been prepared under the guidance of Yamuna, the protagonist of the novel. A young lady with a master's degree in politics, Yamuna is the daughter of Ramji and Rukmini Ammai, a couple known for their devotion to Gandhian ideology and its genuine service to the tribals in Nilgris. We learn that Ramji, in his younger days, was closely associated with Gandhiji and took part in the Champaran Satyagraha, whereas Rukmini Ammai, with whom he fell in love, was an inmate of Gandhiji's Sevagram Ashram. Now, the idealistic couple continue to look after the downtrodden living around the ashram with parental care and affection. Though disillusioned to some extent, they don't seem to have completely lost their faith in a non-violent society, based on the principle of love and established by the means of non-violence.

The function is attended by the elderly Joseph, who is called Ammavan (uncle) by Yamuna, whose upbringing was entrusted to him at a very early age by his parents, since the latter spent most of their time taking care of the Irular children. The other important person taking part in the ashram performance is Dhurai, a Harijan youth and unemployed engineering graduate, who, because of his sterling character, has won the hearts of the inmates of the ashram. When the largely attended show comes to a successful close, he proposes a vote of thanks at the request of Yamuna.

Kamalamma, related to Yamuna through the latter's Keralite mother, invites her to spend the night at her house at Ooty. The stay there proves a turning point in the life of Yamuna because she comes to feel that her early love for Sutir, Kamalamma's son, cannot last long as he has become a hard-core Marxist after his return from the West. In a moving encounter between the two, he ridicules Gandhian ideals and advocates the need for violent methods if the poor in India are to progress. When Yamuna's appeal to him to accept the non-violent path falls on his deaf ears, she feels thoroughly shaken. But her later meeting with her ammavan clears her doubts as he exhorts her to devote her attention to teaching the children in the schools who have to be caught young and exposed to Gandhian principles. With this intention, she goes to her father's elder brother at the city of Madras the sight of which is repulsive to the lady cherishing the virtues of simplicity and brought up in extremely humble surroundings by her parents and foster-father.

After she leaves home, it does not take too long for her to come across men and women of diverse political hues : congressmen, communists, terrorists, anarchists, communalists, separatists and language fanatics. During the journey from Coimbatore to Madras, Yamuna meets one of her former schoolmates, Aruna, who is now a prominent professional speaker and propagandist of Dravida Munnetra Kazhagam. Yamuna is surprised at the other lady's obsession with propaganda and her immense faith in false rhetoric and meaningless rhymes and alliterations. The first one Yamuna meets on her arrival at the city is a young man of a different type. Indunath, a youth Congress leader, captivated by her appearance and intelligence, urges her to join politics and promises to help her through the corridors of power. In is not difficult for her to realize the hollowness of an immature politician who is after power and position and ready to resort to evil means. Her cup of sorrow is full when she becomes an eye-witness to the fall of a party which once enjoyed the privilege of being guided by Gandhiji himself. Gandhiji recognized no hiatus between private morality and public policy, between politics and ethics. But to the present day politicians she comes across, they are two different entities.

The behaviour of Yamuna's periyappa (father's elder brother) is a rude shock to her inasmuch as he happens to be a weather cock and a pretender doing lip service to Gandhian ideology and leading a life of pomp and luxury. His daughter's daughter, Niru, is a stupid young girl enamoured of all the trivialities of life. About to be married to an I.A.S. officer, she spends her time dreaming happy dreams. Yamuna is irritated by the entire family's supreme indifference to the poverty all around. When her periyappa speaks ill of her mother and her ammavan, she decides to leave the place. His treatment of Dhurai, who comes there to reveal the happy news of having got a job in Calcutta, quickens her departure. She cannot forgive her uncle for forgetting Gandhi's assertion that untouchability is the greatest blot on Hinduism.

Yamuna and Dhurai, on their return to the ashram, are informed of their parents desire that they should get married. Dhurai is moved by the extraordinary gesture of the family when Yamuna expresses no objection to her mother's plan. Immediately after the wedding, they go to Calcutta which is torn by riots and violent clashes engineered by extremist groups. The heart-rending scene of suffering multitudes in the dirty slums of the old city has a terrible impact on Yamuna who, horrified by the situation, has no heart for even conjugal bliss and feels guilty in the company of Dhurai. Haunted by inferiority complex and puzzled by Yamuna's indifference, Dhurai starts ill-treating her. Her attempts to assist poor children and helpless women lead to disastrous consequences. She firmly believes that all physical pleasures are unjust and unethical when one is in the midst of the numerous men and women who struggle in vain for the basic needs of life. An average human being with all the characteristic ambitions, desires and weaknesses, Dhurai fails to understand her thoughts and feelings and feels slighted. Her agony knows no bounds when a young boy seeking shelter in her house is brutally attacked by miscreants. Dhurai goes into raptures over his transfer to Patna but she contends that she is sheepishly running away from the place which demands her continued presence and courageous service.

Finally, she agrees to go to Patna where the situation seems worse. The widening gulf between the shameless rich and the exploited poor unnerves her and she begins to question if Gandhiji's ideology is of any practical use in a world where it is impossible to have many mahatmas. Her visit to Mataji's palatial residence is a rude revelation of the kind of life led by the former votaries of Gandhian philosophy who have now tasted political power. As the wife of an ex-minister, Mataji seems to have forgotten all that she learnt about simplicity and other ideals in the ashrams in her younger days along with Yamuna's parents even though in her conversations she recalls those times with a feigned sigh. Yamuna is too stunned to seek her assistance in alleviating the hardships of the poor in their locality. While returning to her house, she comes across Indunath and for courtesy's sake invites him home. He goes to her place that very evening and on finding her alone attempts to rape her but is driven away by her timely action.

Yamuna's faith in mankind gradually gets eroded and she often wonders if the country can ever be redeemed. She is pained to notice that Dhurai, instead of sharing her concern for the weak and the suppressed takes to evil ways and even mocks at her for stubbornly upholding Gandhian ideals. He smokes, drinks, wears expensive clothes, buys plenty of foreign goods and does not hesitate to beat Yamuna when she destroys a few bottles of wine he has brought home. Her ammavan comes to know of her plight, consoles her and urges her not to lose heart and never stray away from the path of love on any account. But soon another tragic occurrence puts her patience to test. While Dhurai is attending a cocktail party in a rich man's bungalow, a bomb is thrown by some revolutionaries and he loses his right foot. In the hospital she tries to cheer him up but he uses harsh words that hurt her. On being told that she is with child, he heartlessly asks her to get rid of it. Though her grief is beyond measure, she takes a decision to bear all miseries without any complaint and to face the ordeal of life boldly. To Gandhiji *Sarvodaya* was no mere dream but something that could be realized here and now. But the unscrupulous politicians and the self-seeking men from the middle class families of the post-colonial India are ready to dismiss all his views as impractical ideals.

Employing profound characters and simple incidents the novel presents an inconclusive debate on the various aspects of Gandhian philosophy and its relevance today. Its matchless beauty lies in its realistic and dispassionate account of the social and political histories of India in the late sixties of the twentieth century. It doesn't boldly assert its acceptance or repudiation of Gandhian ideology. Nor does it claim that the country can solve its problems only by adhering stubbornly to Gandhian principles. It doesn't argue that though much of what Gandhiji advocated may not be practicable today, there is a dire need to inject Gandhian idealism into the blood of our young men and women. It simply bemoans the fact that Gandhism is no more a live force in the country of its birth. It only laments that the truth about Gandhi the man and his message of hope have simply been forgotten.

Does the novel succeed as a critique on Gandhian world-view if it is meant to be one? It cannot because the Gandhian spirit is all too pervasive in the novel. The young lady waging her desperate struggle to uphold the ideals may be shaken in her faith and may find herself in depressed moods time and again. The dark forces may appear to be victorious in their conscious choice of unfair means. Many who have chosen the Gandhian path might fall on the wayside. There is at least one character which carries on cheerfully from beginning to end as a true Gandhian without at any time entertaining any doubts about the relevance or validity of such a role. That is Joseph, Yamuna's foster-father, her ammavan, one of the most successful creations of Rajam Krishnan. A Keralite admirer of Jayaprakash Narayan and a devoted sarvodaya worker, he continues to be stubbornly Gandhian in a world pitted against such people and does his service both as a humble individual shunning publicity and as an animator of Gandhian activities cheering up even the most frustrated beings. Another factor that works against our reading of the novel as an expression of the author's disillusionment with Gandhism is Rajam Krishnan's Gandhian view of art, which is borne out by *Verukku Nir* and other writings of hers. Following in the footsteps of Tolstoy and Ruskin, Gandhiji asserted that all true art must help the soul to realize its inner self. Totally opposed to any opulent rhetoric and to any conscious attempt to excite passions or to resort to any thing merely to please, Gandhiji, unlike the other English-educated, foreign-trained leaders of his time, forged for himself a spare, simple, transparent style. And this is the model Rajam Krishnan as writer has set before herself.

NOTES AND REFERENCES

1. K.R. Srinivasa Iyengar, *Indian Writing in English*, New Delhi : Sterling Publishers Private Limited, 1983, p. 396.
2. Jawaharlal Nehru, *The Discovery of India*, London, 1946, p. 303.
3. K.R. Srinivasa Iyengar, *Indian Writing in English*, p. 397.
4. Raja Rao, *Kanthapura*, 1938, reprint, New Delhi : Orient Paperbacks, 1970, p. 183.
5. Quoted in K.R. Srinivasa Iyengar, *Indian Writing in English*, p. 269.
6. *Ibid*., p. 293.

22

Conflict between Feudalism and Humanism : Thakazhi's *Scavenger's Son* and *Two Measures of Rice*

N. GOPALAKRISHNAN NAIR

The Contribution made by Thakazhi Sivasankara Pillai, in making Malayalam fiction, a powerful instrument of social transformation, has been widely appreciated. His pioneering efforts to break away from the traditional concepts of fictional literature, to initiate the new generation of writers, into a literary and cultural renaissance have been widely acclaimed. With the emergence of the new trend set by Thakazhi, Malayalam fiction turned to the analysis of contemporary social realities. A profound consciousness of the turbulent inner self underlying the apparent human condition exercised a powerful influence in developing on his part a strong conviction that the novelist's primary concern is to react to contemporary life.

By nature and temperament Thakazhi was highly sensitive to any thing that affronts human dignity and denies social justice. Endowed with superior moral sense and profound sympathy for the poorer and the lowly as he was, he could not tolerate any kind of hypocrisy, oppression and exploitation. Perhaps the most powerful influence on Thakazhi, as he has admitted was that of the times. He observed :

> If the literary contributions made by me so far have any significance of social concern, it was due to the influence of the particular conditions of the times when I began to write consciously... Many a story written by me during that period was based on the economic and social justice.[1]

He was born in the village of Thakazhi, a part of Kuttanad, the water locked complex in the delta where Pamba, Manimala and other rivers flow into the back waters, a place with peculiar geographical conditions and economic identity. The place is distinct from other parts of Kerala. What Thakazhi saw, in his early years, around him, was a nightmare of appalling poverty, social discrimination and exploitation of the unprivileged classes.

When Thakazhi began his literary career, he was aware of the changes taking place in the social, political, literary and even domestic scenes all over India. His high moral standards and disturbed sensibilities forced him to highlight the subhuman existence of a large section of people with a view to accelerating the social transition. As K. Ayyappa Paniker stated, "His chief concern in all his work has been the common man, the suffering man the man, discriminated against".[2] His fictional world is the society in which the author and his characters live. His social environment is constantly changing events. What he reveals is an interaction of the society on individual and of the individual on society. His novels have always been a source of guidance to people, making them aware of the values of life. They have inspired the masses to fight for the betterment of human conditions.

The novels *Thottiyude Makan* (Scavenger's Son, 1994) and *Rantidangazhi* (Two Measures of Rice, 1949) give an unbearable picture of what was wrong with the age old establishment and values which were supporting the social structure of the State. They also show how the seeds of destruction of the society emerge from the social structure itself.

By the time Thakazhi wrote *Thottiyude Makan* and *Rantidangazhi* he had acquired technical virtuosity and maturity of expression as a creative artist. His association with political organizations especially with the Travancore State Congress and Communist movement made him aware of the labour movement and the obstacles which the trade unionists had to face in the forties and fifties. He had witnessed the failure of the trade unions on account of psychological and sociological reasons. Lack of class consciousness coupled with age old subjugation to richer classes, and upper castes made them subservient and incapable of undertaking any organizational work. However, Indian national movement and the success of Russian revolution and similar movements the world over resulted in the formulation of certain radical organizations in India, and this tendency was reflected in Kerala first in industrial sectors in the form of trade unions and gradually it spread to other sectors. The subsequent social movement can be expressed in the words of K. Ayyappa Paniker :

> The mass rebellion at Punnapra and Vayalar under the leadership of the Communist party against the repressive force of C.P. Ramaswami Iyyer, then Diwan of Travancore was a violent expression of the pent-up energies of the people of those villages. It was also the unambiguous declaration by the working classes that times had changed.[3]

Thottiyude Makan

Thottiyude Makan (Scavenger's Son) covers three generations of Scavengers, Ishukkumuthu, his son Chudalamuthu and his son Mohanan. Ishukkumuthu who had served the Alleppe municipal town for thirty years could not earn anything except ill-health. His wife had died when his only son Chudalamuthu was a small child. Now, Chudalamuthu is old enough to take up the work, but he does not like the detestable work of a scavenger. However, he is forced to take up the work when his father falls ill. When his father dies, Chudalamuthu cannot find the money required for the burial. The dead body is buried in the night soil depot, from where it is pulled out by dogs. His father's experiences turn out to be a lesson to Chudalamuthu. So, he cherishes the ambition of moving up the social scale. He keeps himself away from the fellow scavengers. Bribing the municipal overseer, Kesava Pillai, he gets into the good books of the authorities. Once he happens to sign a notice appealing the fellow scavengers to organize a trade union. But when there are signs of the union becoming a reality he backs out leaving the fellow scavengers in utter confusion. He secretly meets the overseer, makes deal with him to break the trade union, in return for certain favours for himself. He turns out to be a veritable black leg. Since his marriage with Valli his only interest in life becomes money making. He becomes a money lender. His customers are the fellow scavengers from whom he collects a high rate of interest.

Pichandi, a close friend of Chudalamuthu's father tries to organize a trade union. Naturally the task of foiling it is entrusted with Chudalamuthu, who takes the municipal president in full confidence and hands over all his savings with him in the hope that he will return it when he has enough money to buy a plot and construct a house. Chudalamuthu resorts to all foul means to discredit Pichandi. He spreads rumours that Pichandi has committed theft. At last Pichandi goes away from Alleppey leaving his wife and children destitute. The second attempt of the scavengers to organize a union is foiled.

Chudalamuthu's wife gives birth to a child. He names it Mohanan, a name which won't look like that of a scavenger. When he grows up he is sent to school. But quite against his will Mohanan makes friends with the children of scavengers. Chudalamuthu realises that the money entrusted with the president is lost.

There is an epidemic of cholera among the scavengers. They die in large numbers. Fresh recruits of scavengers are brought from Thirunelveli. Chudalamuthu is appointed to supervise the burial of the scavengers who die of cholera. He and his wife die of cholera. Mohanan grows up as a beggar in the company of the children of scavengers. They all become scavengers and organize powerful trade unions, capable of striking work and organizing processions. They develop class consciousness.

Chudalamuthu's story is a discord between person and circumstances. He is not allowed to escape the confines of his enclosed living and realize his yearnings. His tragedy lies in the frustration of his high aspiration to make his son something other than a scavenger :

> He wanted his son not to become a scavenger. A name different from those of scavengers was given to him. He grew up without knowing who is a scavenger. When that child was found lying in its excreta his father got agitated. But, today he is a scavenger in the town of Alleppey. When the members of the upper caste came to know that his name was Mohanan, they frowned.[4]

The social and moral implications of this description of the protagonist's plight are quite clear. The irony of the tragic situations of Chudalamuthu is that despite all his individual qualities and aspirations he is denied opportunity to make use of his potentialities to make his dreams a reality.

The main thrust of the novel is to highlight the individual

qualities of the protagonist set against the subhuman quality of the life lived by him. By accident of his low birth and the socio-economic compulsions, he takes up the job of cleaning latrines. The inhuman treatment of the poor by the upper class is illustrated by Kesava Pillai, the overseer. Through him the author makes a severe indictment of capitalist callousness. His attitude towards the scavengers at the time of the epidemic of smallpox is a typical example of the ruthlessness and duplicity and social maneuvering of the people of his class. He turns down the instruction of the municipal president to vaccinate the scavengers against smallpox, saying "it is high time that these scavengers are changed. Moreover, think of the present time. Though the union is broken they are hankering after it. Again, union may be formed."[5] Here Kesava Pillai represents a cynical disregard for all norms or codes of civilized humanity. He thinks that the epidemic will eliminate the entire lot of scavengers, so that the trade unions too will go along with them. Even the municipal president, who represents the capitalist values is a little moved at the suggestion of Kesava Pillai. He asks :

> "Aren't they also human beings? Haven't they got children and babies?" The question provokes Kesava Pillai to make one of his most sarcastic and inhuman comments :
>
> "Are they human beings? fine."[6]

Rantidangazhi (*Two Measures of Rice*)

Rantidangazhi, one of the best works of socialist realism in Indian fiction is a comprehensive picture of the historical process of the awakening of millions of our farmers. It is centered round the social transformation brought about by the breakdown of the old social order and the emergence of modern industrial culture. This change in social patterns is better expressed in Thakazhi's words :

> In 1922, the Punnapra Vayalar struggle transformed agriculture into an industry, I could see reflections of that change in my father who was a farmer. This change brought about a revolution in the relationship between the farmer and the agricultural labourer. It is to tell this that I have written the *Two Measures of Rice*.[7]

The major concern of Thakazhi is to dramatise the breakdown of the old order by the industrialization of agriculture. The spirit of co-operation and the feeling of a larger family that governed the relation between the landlords and farm labourers are lost as a result of the emergence of commercial values.

The novel *Rantidangazhi* (Two Measures of Rice) has a simple plot. Chirutha the daughter of Kalipulayan and Kunjali has the reputation of being an excellent farmhand. So, Kalipulayan demands a handsome brideprice for her. Chathan and Koran aspire her hand. Chathan fails to fulfil the demands of Kalipulayan. But Koran who is an enterprising man becomes the bonded labourer of Pushpavelil Ouseph and secures enough money and rice to marry Chirutha.

Ouseph's hundred acres of rice field is given to the charge of Koran who works hard to make that year's yield the best in the whole locality. He achieves the target and feels proud of being a good farm labourer. He hopes that he would get a handsome share of the harvest, and become a permanent worker of Ouseph. But to his great disappointment he is given only a meagre wage instead of his due share, and is disposed of like other labourers. He has no sufficient courage to question the injustice meted out on him.

Koran now becomes aware of the change in socio-political scenario. He is aware of trade unions sectors. He tries to organize a trade union of the farm laboures. This invites the wrath of the landowners. They express it at the time of the death of Koran's father. They do not allow Koran to bury the dead body in the land where he lived. This incident makes him devoted more to the trade union.

One day, Chacko, Ouseph's son, tries to molest Chirutha. Incidentally Koran appears on the scene and a scuffle follows. Chacko is killed. Convicted of murder, Koran is sentenced for fifteen years of imprisonment. Koran entrusts Chathan, his friend and former lover of his wife with the care of Chirutha, who is pregnant. Chathan looks after her with brotherly devotion. Chirutha gives birth to a child. Chathan helps her to bring him up. When the term of imprisonment of Koran comes to an end he joins his friend Chathan, his wife Chirutha and the child. Their sufferings are not in vain. They see a new generation of workers who are free to organize, shout slogans and bargain for higher wages and better working conditions.

The main thrust of both the novels is the human situation resulting from the separation of man from his society. Presenting this situation through the predicaments of the major characters of the two novels, Thakazhi tries to bring this theme into sharper focus and broadens his concern from the individual to their community as a whole. In doing so he seeks ultimately to express the aspirations and basic problems of all such social rejects and projects the general social crisis of the period. This is evident from what Thakazhi says about all such victims of the society towards the end of *Scavenger's Son* :

> Look back. How many millions of Chudalamuthus and Vallies have been crushed to punish like this! How many thousands of years it has been happening! Where shall their aspirations, dreams, loves, hatred and all join other than this atmosphere.[8]

The picture of the wretched existence of the lowclass people in both the novels is similar. Their life is one of ruin and misery caused by poverty, exploitation, debt forced labour and eviction from their dwellings. In *Two Measures of Rice*, the description of Koran's father is typical of the common plight of the agricultural labourers of the rich rice fields of Kuttanad :

> He had groped his way to his son's to spend his last days there with him. He wanted to drink Kanji — his last wish! He was only a boy of eight when he joined as a farm hand in the service of a big farmer who had about two thousand acres of paddy field. Since then that farmer had become a millionaire... How many millions of bushels of grain has he produced in sixty-two years of life as farm worker! How many harvests he had gathered, what mountain of grain he had threshed! How many millions of people were fed from the fruits of this old man's labour! What a magnificent contribution to human life he had made!... And now here he was dragging helplessly the burden of his own miserable life through the last chapters of his earthly existence!.[9]

The novel bears an eloquent testimony to the ruin and misery suffered by the farm labourers and poor farmers. The portrayal of the tragic situation is not an end in itself. The purpose of the author to expose the force responsible for the prevalence of such a situation is to rouse the moral indignation of a larger section of the society leading to the spirit of proper reaction. The spirit of such revolutionary awakening in the agricultural labourers of Kuttanad is depicted by Thakazhi :

> Hunger began to goad the Pulayas — the men who could toil without respite in the water, who could expose themselves to the burning sun or bitter cold, or biting wind. They failed to understand that the latent might of the Pulayas — whom the elements could not subdue was being awakened.[10]

In these novels Thakazhi presents the central theme of social revolution mainly through the portrayal of the heroes. In *Rantidangazhi* the social changes bring about a class consciousness on the part of the hero and he becomes a revolutionary, whereas in *Scavenger's Son* the hero falls into the hands of the capitalist forces and becomes their instrument to break the unions. However, the union of both the sectors becomes a reality at the end of the novels.

These novels present a Marxist interpretation of the social situation. One may think that *Scavenger's Son* is a social analysis in terms of Marxian theory of dialectical materialism and economic determinism. Caste figures only as a social factor to create the social situation. The protagonist's social environment is made up of capitalist forces. He thinks that the capitalist system of the society is the root cause of the prevalence of untouchability. Characters like Kesava Pillai manipulate the prevailing socio-economic systems for their benefit and suppress the workers' ambitions. This is a definite illustration of how capitalism in the form of such callous human beings replaces social and moral values by what Marx termed cash-nexus.

Thottiyude Makan (Scavenger's Son) and *Rantidangazhi* (Two Measures of Rice) are companion volumes, which can be compared to the fictional achievements of Mulk Raj Anand in *Untouchable* and *Coolie* and that of Premchand in *Karma Bhoomi* and *Godan*. Like Premchand and Anand, Thakazhi's major interest in his fictional writings was to draw a true picture of the class struggle and the resultant emergence of a new social order. The unique contributions made by Thakazhi through his fictional literature for the realization of the new social order will ever be remembered.

REFERENCES

1. Thakazhi Sivasankara Pillai, "Ente Kathayezhuthinte Balyam", The Childhood of My Story Writing, *Ekantha Pathikan*, The Lone Traveller, Quilon : Manjusha, 1969, p. 11.
2. K. Ayyappa Paniker, *Thakazhi Sivasankara Pillai*, Trivandrum : University of Kerala, 1988, p. 136.
3. *Ibid*., p. 77.
4. Thakazhi Sivasankara Pillai, *Scavenger's Son* Translation of Thottiyude Makan by R.E. Asher, New Delhi : Orinet Longman, 1974, p. 168.
5. *Scavenger's Son*, p. 73.
6. *Ibid*., p. 74.
7. T.N. Jayachandran, *Novelistinte Silpasala*. The Novelist's Workshop, Kottayam : SPCS, 1970, p. 34.
8. *Scavenger's Son*, p. 167.
9. Thakazhi Sivasankara Pillai, *Two Measures of Rice*, Translation of *Rantidangazhi* by M.A. Shakoor, Bombay : Jaico, 1967, p. 79.
10. *Two Measures of Rice*, p. 81.

23

Conservatism Versus Progress : Ramakrishnan's *Verukkal*

M. MURALI GANAM

To make a thorough assessment and a contribution of the contemporary novel in Malayalam is a painstaking effort in itself for the simple reason that the Malayalam novel very much like the short story, or drama or literary criticism has always been the prototype of English patterns, but suited to its own sensibility and style. The novel of its kind in Malayalam came into being in 1887 with Nedungadi's *Kundalata* a novel with an inbuilt suspense tale (presumably with the influence of Walter Scott) was an attempt to capture the comprehensive view of life in general. This was followed by the emergence of eminent writers like Chandu Menon and Raman Pillai who established their prominence in the field of Malayalam fiction with their realistic pictures of contemporary society with all its deformities.

And although this was followed by a general lull in the output of good function owing to the fact of a neglect in the output of social novels, the likes of contemporary writers like Thakazhi, Kesadev, Basheer and Pottekat revived the social purpose in the Malayalam novel.

Malayatoor Ramakrishnan's *Verukkal* seeks to portray the life of the orthodox brahmin community, the conventions and superstitions, and all those passions which man is heir to as its main disconcerting reality. It is in the first few pages of the novel that we are introduced to a socially relevant theme of an unhappy matrimonial alliance caused by social inequality. The story is simple enough.

Iyer an I.A.S. Officer hailing from an orthodox brahmin family is wedded to Geetha, daughter of a business tycoon settled in Madras. Geetha is easily discerned as the symbol of the flawed and upcoming new generation depending solely on material possession and comforts. Her material aspiration of building their new house on a four thousand five hundred square feet land is all that her consciousness can retain as she insists that her husband either sells his ancestral land to make up the sum for the purchase, or accept in all humility financial assistance from her rich father. The latter choice is however unacceptable to Raghu, as he fights to retain his identity in the social mileau and at home, and it is in the clash between the forces of the new and the old, between progress and blind conservatism that Malayatoor Ramakrishnan portrays in vividness the language of basic human values and emotions.

The conflict is serially arranged and logically developed through many episodes unwinding itself that the reader is forced to survey the whole scene dispassionately and comprehensively to understand the precipice of social and moral degradation. Thus, it is with Raghu's acceptance of the challenge to sever his ties with his ancestral property (that includes his blood relatives, his sisters Ammulu and Lakshmi) that the conflict becomes inevitable, as people of different temperaments and traditions are brought together to unfold in realistic detail the novel's essential meaning. Beginning with Raghu's recapitulation of the mango episode in Paata's compound, marks, the beginning of a fresh journey not only into the novel's past, but the journey of the mind of the reader to infinity and back :

> "As they neared the gate, there was the sound of something falling. A mango had fallen on the bonnet of the car. The 'grandpa' mango tree near the gate had not forgotten to bear fruit this year also. The falling mango unfurled more memories of the past."[1]

There is an undercurrent of sorrow in what Karthavu the manager of Mana tells Raghu regarding the latter's disposal of his ancestral property which can also be considered as a stark criticism of modern society, its hypocrisy, selfishness and easy evasions :

> What news can there be, here of all places? When man has reached the moon and is conquering space, people

> here have not been able to get for themselves even the smallest facilities. Look at the road here. Has anyone felt, upto this day, that it should be repaired? During the monsoons it is like a ploughed up field. How are the children to walk to the distant school? In summer the road is unbearably dusty. Is there a doctor? Or a hospital? Leave alone that, is there even a good ayurvedic physician? That some of our villagers celebrate their eightieth and ninetieth birthdays is one of the minor wonders. The people here would never unite for a common purpose. They have no enthusiasm.[2]

In the above lines one sees Ramakrishnan's views as a strong critic of society who analyses the individual and finds him wanting not only in individual responsibility but sensibility as well. And that he sees and feels as a member of society he translates into his novel to expose the basic contradictions that characterise life everywhere. But the tragedy is man sees it all with a pained heart but does little to better his conditions and allows endless rivalries, infinite misery, hunger, disease, jealousy and struggle for power to eat up his life's sustenance. It is this atmosphere of sheer helplessness as one sees that envelops the majority of the characters in *Verukkal*.

Another instance of a social awakening is not only witnessed but relieved by the reader in going through the episode of Raghu's outright protest against the social myths and untouchability of the day :

> "The episode concerned the temple, which was the private property of the Namboodiri Mana. Only caste Hindus could make obeisance only from a distance and put their offerings into a box kept outside the temple walls. Right from the time Raghu came to the village he had felt that this kind of untouchability was not right. He had kept his moral indignation to himself."[3]

This plainly reveals that life for Raghu (just as for the author) is something to be fought for and lived out in its entirety. It is precisely in what man has made of man at the end of it all that grieves Raghu and forces him to look at society as a tyrannical machine. Man is left with but only one choice; to smash it, if he does not want man to be pulverised under its wheels. And this is what Raghunath Iyer the once timid brahmin boy sets out to do in the role of a social worker.

Although the story itself is built on many superstitions, the conflict in the novel reaches its peak with the arrival of Devassy the toddy shop owner (whose attempt to purchase the ancestral land) sends Raghu reeling into a new level of awareness as he realises to his horror that disposal of his ancestral land would not only plunge him in greater agony but would be simply ignoring his father's greatest sacrifice for him :

> "If only you had got good medicines and proper treatment, would you not have been with me today? But your medicines were confined to two measures of 'Dhanwanthram' herbal massage oil and handfuls of chonnamuki leaves. How many things did you abjure to spend on my education, to see that money was sent to me regularly. You even gave up proper treatment for your illness."[4]

The situation becomes unbearable in Raghu's mind as he fights to ward off temptations to sell his land and finally emerges victorious when it dawns on him that his ancestral land was :

> "Not just an item of property, or a mere house and compound but an entire tradition."[5]

> "His roots were in this piece of land. They were in this ancient soil. What a fool he had been not to realise it. Hadn't he tried to cut off his own roots. Ammulu had been to no school but she knew where the roots of men and women lay. The roots of man and the roots of trees were in the earth, in the soil."[6]

To conclude it may be stated that although Malayatoor Ramakrishnan's novels are deliberately designed to expose the rots which corrode society, there is that uncommon vitality in his idioms, plots and characters that are not only forceful but have a thought-provoking quality as well. The subject matter of his fiction may be with the circumstances of the society which gave him birth but his digs at the foibles of that society reveal a certain measure of purposefulness, and that is why there are no elaborate plots in his novels — in fact they are short stories elongated, but the characters presented by him as playing their preordained roles in the drama of life are so expertly drawn that they are as significant as any in much bigger works which permit enough room for their fuller delineation.

REFERENCES

1. Ramakrishnan Malayatoor, *Verukkal*, 1985 : Madras, Macmillan, p. 26.
2. *Ibid.*, p. 97.
3. *Ibid.*, p. 115.
4. *Ibid.*, p. 130.
5. *Ibid.*, p. 131.
6. *Ibid.*, p. 118.

24

A Dreadful Plight of an Untouchable : Shivaram Karanth's *Choma's Drum*

VIJAYA GUTTAL

Karanth occupies a place of unique significance in the tradition of the novel form in Kannada literature. Before him the novel was mainly characterised by works which were religious and didactic on the one hand, and patriotic on the other. Karanth began a new tradition of his own and focussed on the fundamental concerns of human existence in the most realistic manner in his novels. Unlike earlier writers, he was able to penetrate into the vexing contemporary social problems of the poor and the downtrodden, their deprivation, and exploitation and present them in the larger context of the human predicament. L.S. Sheshagiri Rao aptly writes, "Kannada was singularly fortunate that this titan appeared so early in the history of fiction, for straightaway it developed adult interests. And to him the novel is a responsibility, a way of probing and evaluating experience. He is intensely moral without being didactic. He is singularly free from sentimentality."[1] Among the various thematic patterns he develops, one of the most significant is the portrayal of the social evils. It is presented in *Choma's Drum* in all its depth and complexity without any touch of propaganda. To bring about a social revolution is not really his purpose. His commitment is to reflect truthfully the exploitative nature of man and the resultant human misery. The world of his novels is characterised by a deep sense of humanity, complex view of life, realistic approach and a strong social consciousness.

Choma's Drum is an important novel of Karanth in which he deals with the tragic implications of untouchability in the most moving manner. Comparing *Choma's Drum* to Mulk Raj Anand's

Untouchable, both of which belong to the 1930s, Prof. G.S. Amur points out that both writers choose the point of view of an untouchable to criticise a caste-ridden, conservative society.[2] Such a technique lends authenticity and urgency to the picture portrayed. Further Prof. Amur says that *Untouchable* is a realistic novel influenced by the philosophy of Marx.[3] The significance of Karanth's novel does not stop at being merely a socio-political novel like *Untouchable*, but extends to become a profoundly complex novel that portrays reality with all its paradoxical dimensions.[4] It creates in Choma a memorable character who at once stands as a helpless victim and also a powerful symbol of silent protest.

Choma's Drum is relatively a short novel in which the action is extremely concentrated without any deviation and the narration moves swiftly to the depiction of the basic issues. At the very outset Choma is introduced through his drum beat which almost echoes the beat of his heart. It is Choma's character which holds the various threads of the story together. In spite of the fact that he is an untouchable and utterly poor, he cherishes one overwhelming aspiration in his life, that is to become a farmer and till his own land. He is aware that in the society in which he lives untouchables are not allowed to own land; yet he clings to the hope that some day he would plough his own land. It is a dream and an aspiration for the realisation of which he has been rearing a pair of young bullocks he had found, lost in the forest. The plough stands as a symbol of his secret hopes. Finally Choma musters his courage and puts forth his request to his master Sankappayya, the brahmin zamindar of the village. He pleads most abjectly, saying even if Sankappayya gives him a useless piece of land for rent he would be grateful.

Really Sankappayya is not averse to giving Choma unused land. But his old mother is set against the idea because such a thing has never been done before and she thinks it is sheer arrogance on the part of Choma, an untouchable, to aspire to be a farmer. Choma begs Sankappayya for land, hoping for a change of mind, not once but three times in the novel and on all occasions the answer is in the negative, leaving Choma heart-broken. At one moment, in defiance, he thinks of trying to acquire government land, but he is also afraid of losing, by that, the regular wages he gets from Sankappayya. If he fails to grow anything, then he will be left with no means of sustenance. His frustration at the way he is hemmed in on all sides makes him numb with despair, but yet he cannot forego his deepest desire. Sometimes his inner fury breaks out into reckless beating of the drum. On one occasion in a fit of drunken frenzy he almost breaks the front legs of his oxen thinking if he cannot use them for himself, why should they be used in the service of others.[5] Choma is not an intellectual; the only way he knows to pour his heart out is to get drunk and beat the drum. His frenzied beating of the drum is his silent protest against the cruel order of things which he cannot change.

The root cause of his sorrow and poverty is seen in his being an untouchable. In his comparison of Anand's novel *Untouchable* and *Choma's Drum* Prof. Amur points out that in both novels the one thing that creates insurmountable obstacles is the caste-based untouchability.[6] The society which upholds these inhuman customs, dead ideas and rituals of religion comes under a severe attack. Choma becomes a representative of a whole section of individuals who had become nonentities and whose potential had remained unrealised because they are inescapably trapped by the society like Choma.

The fictional world of the novel is divided into two parts which are skillfully woven together to make it a coherent whole. On the one hand, there is the village world of Bhoganahalli which opposes all change. The rigidity of its social reality is represented by Sankappayya's old mother and Sankappayya's own unquestioning acceptance of that reality. On the other hand we have the modern world of the Coffee estate of Michael where the poor labourers, mostly all untouchables, treated like cattle and systematically exploited. The agents like Manvel tempt, cajole and threaten the ignorant labourers and force them to come to work away from their homes in the inhuman conditions of the Coffee garden.

A popular belief among the labourers aptly describes the conditions "The fever and debt once contracted at the coffee estate can never be got rid of".[7] The five rupee debt of Choma has risen to twenty in five years, in Manvel's words, to return which Choma is forced to send two of his eldest sons. That is the beginning of the tragic break-up of his family. His younger son Guruva gets converted to Christianity and marries a Christian girl. The eldest son Chaniya returns home but dies soon after from the fever caught at the coffee garden. Later on Belli, Choma's daughter, who goes to work as a labourer to return the yet unsettled debt becomes a victim of the sexual exploitation of Michael and Manvel. The world of the coffee estate exploits the labourers economically and dehumanises them, as the world of Bhoganahalli exploits them in the name of religion. Both these worlds shake Choma's faith, life and render existence devoid of meaning.

The tragedy of Choma reaches its climax when he comes face to face with the terrible reality of being an untouchable on the occasion of his youngest son Nila's death. When the boy is drowning in the pond the people around refuse to help to save him because he is an untouchable. Then "Choma realised fully that the life of an untouchable is like a running sore" (XVII). Choma takes away his son's body to the hut and shuts himself up inside numbed by grief. The next morning he buries the body unseen by anyone. Later on he was seen beating the drum mercilessly.

The third refusal of Sankappayya to give him any land coupled with the tragedy of Nila's death intensifies Choma's despair and his faith in all that he has believed in is shaken. He realises that as long as he remains an untouchable his desire to become a farmer will remain unfulfilled. Then he remembers his second son Guruva who is converted and has become a farmer himself. Choma thinks when his own gods have not come to his aid what wrong is there in believing the Christian god. The helpless protest of his soul against his condition is heard when he ruminates, "Instead being an untouchable, if he had belonged to any other caste his Nila would have been saved." He said, "The caste of the untouchables is an unwanted caste even to God. Why does God bring men like him into this life? And why does he torment them?" he asked (XVII). The abject condition of Choma serves as a metaphor for suppression, debasement and servility which are an inescapable part of his life.

Unfortunately Choma's decision to get converted is defeated by his lifelong belief in Panjurli, the god of his ancestors and in the end he decides to face whatever good or evil fate brings staying in the traditional fold. Paradoxically, the peace he makes with his god is broken when he sees Belli with The Christian Manvel. Suddenly the old fury erupts seeing the daughter of his heart betray his faith. His grief and despair reach the breaking point. In a heartrending gesture, Choma decides to cut himself from all ties; he throws Belli out of the hut, leaves the bullocks back in the forest from where they had come, breaks the plough, the symbol of his one overwhelming aspiration in life, to pieces and burns them. Lastly he seizes the drum and beats it with such madness as never before and dies beating the drum as if to make the world hear the agony of his soul's cry. This last scene of Choma's life is a superb work of art which impresses upon us not as a tame acceptance of his tragic fate but as an act of turbulent defiance.

In Choma, Karanth has created one of the most memorable characters in the world of fiction. He seems to share something of the spirit of Hemingway's hero of *The Old Man and the Sea*. Choma too is fighting against great odds and the agonised cry of his heart for freedom from the man-made social shackles is not in vain, for it reverberates in the minds of all the readers. When Choma asks for land, Sankappayya's mother thinks it as a mark of arrogance. Truly, in his very persistence and boldness to aspire to become a farmer against all odds, in this very heroic act on his part, one may see his defiance of the dead customs of a heartless society and the voice of his silent protest. Even when the entire world seems to be set against him, suppressing him, his inner cry is not suppressed. Though Choma himself does not bring about any social revolution or that his defiant act does not have any immediately visible effect, its reaction may be felt long after in the march of social evolution.

The intensity and the genuineness of the suffering of Choma and men like him initiate effects seen much later. It is almost like sowing a seed whose effect, the full-grown tree, is seen years later. From this point of view, Choma's end, though appears like a failure is not really a failure. For his frenzied drum-beating which expresses his inner agony seems to be prophetic, "ringing in" a new dawn. Hence, perhaps it is not really true to say as Prof. Amur does that even if there is a symbolic parallel drawn between *Choma's Drum* and the drum of Shiva, which is itself a symbol of death and destruction, these associations remain part of the inner action of the novel and do not initiate any social movement.[8] The drum of Shiva not only symbolises destruction, the last stage of the universal process, but it also stands for the principle which makes way for new creation. It is implicit in it. Hence, even if any evidence of direct social reaction is absent in *Choma's Drum*, in a larger sense, the novel, through its hero, raises its voice of protest and joins with such others to initiate change. The modern situation in which the descendants of Choma have been able to lift their heads out of the misery of the caste perhaps was made possible through the accumulated sacrifices and agony of such as Choma. The history of mankind shows that the cry of the human soul bears its own fruit in the course of time. Thus, the implications suggested by *Choma's Drum* go beyond any theory of Marxism or even humanism, to provide us a searing picture of the human predicament.

REFERENCES

1. Sheshagiri Rao L.S., *A History of Kannada Literature*, First World Kannada Conference Publication III, Bangalore, 1983, p. 137.
2. Amur G.S., *Kannada Narrative Literature*, Shrihari Prakashana, Dharwad, 1994, p. 105.
3. *Ibid*., p. 106.
4. *Ibid*., p. 116.
5. Karanth Shivaram, *Choma's Drum*, Kannada edition, SBS Publication, Bangalore, Reprint 1992, p. 79.
6. Amur G.S., *op. cit*., p. 108.
7. *Choma's Drum*, *op. cit*., Chapter 3, p. 19.
8. Amur G.S., *op. cit*., p. 117.

25

Ideological Impulsions of the Freedom Struggle : Malathi Chendur's *Hridayanetri*

C.R. VISWESWARA RAO

Malathi Chendur's *Hridayanetri* depicts on a vast canvas the struggle of three generations spanning seven decades in time from Ramudattaiah and Janakamma through Gopalam, the protagonist to Swarajyam, Gopalam's granddaughter. The novel traces how these characters discover their identity as it grows out of their sense of nationality. The urges and aspirations of Ramudattaiah and Janakamma to transform Gandhian ideals into a reality and to usher in a casteless society assuring not only political but social egalitarianism make an indelible imprint on the young mind of Gopalam who seeks, through several failures of approaches to the purpose, to carve out his identity so that it might attune itself to the ideological convictions of Ramudattaiah and thus cohere into a nationality, that collective image or myth used as a frame of reference by which the creative artist's discovery of the ethos is to be judged. In the final resolution offered in *Hridayanetri*, nationality in the post-Independence context seems to be defined not by the rejection of the cultural invasion caused by imperialism but by an assertion of the tradition which upholds the humanistic ideal. Malathi Chendur's treatment of the phenomenon of cultural change and her articulation of the theme of comradeship and communion in a society fast engulfing itself in stultifying materialistic values show her to be a gifted raconteur who, through a weaving of period history, especially of Andhra Pradesh, interlaced with her narrative, offers a vivid picture of a country still in transition and passing through the birth pangs of a new socio-political order.

The novel is dotted with a variety of references to certain vital aspects of the Freedom Struggle and the end of the British Raj it sought, apart from an awakened social conscience it aimed at promoting as a self-imposed pre-condition as it were to self-rule. Ramalakshmamma or Ramudattaiah and her husband Vasudeva Rao, "an Ekalavya disciple of Gandhi," not only wore khadder and boycotted foreign goods but entertained guests whose caste was immaterial to them. Congress was their caste and independence their sole objective. In some of these scenes the novel offers a sustained denunciation of the hierarchy of the caste system and the observance of untouchability. It expounds in its poetics of the uncared for the doctrine of the brotherhood of all men and the equality of castes. In their day-to-day life, and in word, thought, and deed, Ramudattaiah and Vasudeva Rao followed in the footsteps of Gandhi, a fact which filters through the consciousness of Gopalam as he undergoes an ideological apprenticeship, as a foster son as it were, in the new household he enters. The novel contains an implied feminist manifesto when it states the theme of the equality of the sexes and projects emancipated women choosing deliberate, conscious self-abnegation. It is here that Ramudattaiah and Janakamma prove themselves to be the shaping powers at work. In the end, their mantle falls on Gopalam's daughter, Swarajyam, who decides to run a home for the aged in the house bequeathed by Ramudattaiah as a fitting memorial for the selfless, unostentatious sacrifice she symbolizes. Swarajyam's quest for seeking an identity that coheres with her sense of nationality and societal priorities attains fulfilment when she spurns conventional marriage her mother pleads for. She declares thus :

> Marriage is not the only destination for all lives... There are greater ideals. Grandma! I am not running away from home. I shall take you along with me and make the lives of some more elders happy. Is this unacceptable?[1]

It is then that Gopalam realises that Janakamma, hundred years old, is but a diviner of the future. For her the youth are the torchbearers of the country's progressive ideals. It is as though in the vision of her heart she foresaw it all and thus placed on Swarajyam's shoulders the onerous responsibility of interaction with society which fructifies in service to mankind. The stark realities of post-Independence political rulership governed by materialistic aspiration and self-seeking are thus spurned in a rededication in the Gandhian manner to service to the destitute and the underprivileged. This also illustrates the theme of the interconnectedness of the various strands of the poetics of the uncared for.

This is broadly the theme of *Hridayanetri*, a *bildunsroman* which traces the maturity of an idealist through the various stages of temptation and testing and infirmities of purpose to a final commitment to the Gandhian cause. This is exemplified not in terms of an individual taking upon himself an active life lived in the community for its transformation but in terms of a life of detachment, the life of an exemplar. But it is a life which shows itself as a relic of the past and therefore more a representative of the heritage aspired for than something that is productive of a pervasive and wide-spread societal good by itself. Gopalam, even through all his prevarications, represents an irrevocable, inalienable faith in the Gandhian ideals which at times does not stand the test of endurance through the besetting ills of life. When his granddaughter Swarajyam was arrested during the Emergency, he was torn between familial obligations and Gandhian detachment which abjures the use of power as a means of self-sustenance and self-promotion. The means-ends controversy raging within finds its culmination in his utterance to his brother wherein the retreat from Gandhian values becomes evident. Gopalam issues an open threat of digging up skeletons in the cupboard when he says :

> Our ways are different. They don't meet, they can never. I do what I believe in. Your are following your faith. By my faith I may not earn name and fame for the family. Power and pelf may not be at my disposal. I am not sorry for that. But now that it's time let me raise a few questions. "What happened to mother's gold ornaments? Who killed her? I didn't want to but now I am bent on digging up this past" (281-82).

The question here is Gopalam too acts under pressure of circumstances and joins in the retreat from Gandhian values by using blackmail as a potent threat for getting Swarajyam released from prison. This is the post-Emergency situation where Gopalam's unflinching devotion to truth and to adherence to certain norms of public behaviour and private morality seem to be wavering. Perhaps Malathi Chendur implies that in the common man who sought an uncommon tryst with Gandhian destiny, faith in Gandhian ideals is not deep and abiding. At every crucial stage in his life Gopalam seems to waver and finally choose the path of compromise except where of course he rejects the lure of power and thus shows himself to be a contrast to Nandaiah whose rise from humble origins has not invested him with a capacity for selflessness and sacrifice when it came to serving his own community, let alone the larger humanity.

Malathi Chendur is comparable to Nayantara Sahgal in her treatment of the theme of freedom, its value as well as its perils in nascent democracies. Nayantara Sahgal is worth being quoted in this context:

> I think it is worth remembering that freedom means creativity, adventure, experimentation, even risk. I don't believe that these are possible without voluntary choices for action and co-operation.[2]

It is this voluntary choice which Swarajyam makes in the novel by deciding to run a destitute home and thus follow the Gandhian path of service.

In both Malathi Chendur and Nayantara Sahgal the backdrop of the action is provided by the Freedom Movement and the values generated by it. Both the novelists deal with a vast segment of history. Nayantara Sahgal in *Rich Like Us* deals with Indian history in a manner that the entire history from the Mughal period down to contemporary times is telescoped into the narrative. But, while contemporary history provides the events, sometimes thinly disguised, history of the Mughal period suggests symbolically a tale of oppression and torture and the fetters imposed on freedom. The evocative power of the symbol enables the novelist to achieve compression and avoid to some extent the tracing of period history, for when the barriers between history and fiction are broken down the question of the *raison de'tre* of art arises. Without fictionalization and imaginative transmutation of the raw materials of art, what is the distinction that exists between history and fiction? What Balachandra Rajan says in a slightly different context is significant :

> Though social significance may be achieved in the end, it cannot be a requirement of the beginning. This beginning cannot spring from resolutions however carefully drafted, from blueprints however scrupulous, or from inductions from literary performance however cautious and however temperate. The beginning must be where it has always remained — in the creative conscience of the artist and in the struggle for definition which is a condition of that conscience.[3]

When we examine Malathi Chendur in the light of this observation, we seem to feel that *Hridayanetri* offers a rich yield to the historian, by which the work's value as literature cannot be judged. Even in its treatment of history, it is unlike the well-known works, say Scott's *The Heart of Midlothian* or Thackeray's *Henry Esmond.* Nor does it lead up to cyclical view of history wherein a whole culture or a whole way of life, through the pressures of its antiquity, is traced, as in the more recent African fiction, say as in Ngugi or in Armah. Armah focuses on the need for an awakening of the communal imagination. He offers us vistas which take us back to the African past in order to enable us to have a glimpse of the present, and through it a prospect of the future. As Bernth Lindfors observes, Armah possesses a "Janus-like view" which looks forward at the same time as it fixes its gaze on the past. His novels are more in the nature of "visionary myths" than "historical chronicles."[4] Then what filters through the consciousness of Gopalam in *Hridayanetri* is a history of the recent Indian past nostalgically remembered and re-traced (without evidence of any dialogic phonation) not with a view to offering a cultural production but with view to showing certain contrasts and a certain decline in order to highlight the point, like Nayantara Sahgal, that "freedom is just an isolated political achievement for us. It hasn't become a habit of mind or a way of life."[5] In the process, a social purpose and a social consciousness no doubt become evident. But the intensity of the Indianness of the writer in evolving a collective myth for evoking either a picture of a 'wounded civilization' or a civilization showing a capacity for surviving through a 'million mutinies now' seems not much in evidence in *Hridayanetri*.

REFERENCES

1. Malathi Chendur, *Hridayanetri*, Vijayawada : Sri Sailaja Publications, 1991, p. 306. Subsequent references are to this edition.
2. Nayantara Sahgal, "A Search for Answers," *Indian Renaissance* ed. K. Ayyappa Panikar, Delhi : Sterling Publishers, 1983, p. 88.
3. Balachandra Rajan, "Nationality and Identity," *Commonwealth Literature: Unity and Diversity in a Common Culture*, London : Heinemann Educational Books, 1965, p. 22.
4. Bernth Lindfors, "Armah's Histories," *African Literature Today*, No. 11, 1980, p. 86.
5. Nayantara Sahgal, *Storm in Chandigarh*, 1969, Delhi : Hind Pocket Books, 1970, p. 225.

26

Plea for Participation of Women in Politics — Uppala Lakshmana Rao's *Athadu Aame*

K. SREEDEVI

The Telugu novels like *Malapalli* and *Kollayi Gattithe Nemi* have depicted the National movement upto 1922. The novel "Athadu-Aame" (He-She), written by Uppala Lakshmana Rao long after the days of the National movement, has recorded and revived that movement in a detailed and impassioned manner. The author himself participated in the National movement. The novel has not limited itself to depicting the Congress politics. It has also dwelt upon the activities of the Socialist and Communist parties in the days of the National movement, including the secret activities of the revolutionaries against the British Government.

The novelist adopts an innovative style of revealing the whole story from the diaries maintained by the two major characters in the novel. Uppala Lakshmana Rao is successful in creating characters in the novel, whose consciousness truly reflects the contemporary social conditions. These characters express their reactions to the contemporary economic, political and social questions. The writer's own understanding of the political, economic and social problems of the day find their reflection in the diaries maintained by the characters.

The story of the novel runs thus : After enrolling as Barrister in England, Sastri returns to Madras. Shantham a young lady, after her studies in Economics, joins Queen Mary's College as a lecturer. They fall in love with each other and got their marriage registered.

After the marriage Shantham gives up the job. She gives shelter to a girl of fifteen who has run away from her parents. This girl loves Janardhan and marries him. By now, Shantham and Sastri have their own daughter, Lakshmi who inherits all the good physical and mental qualities of her parents. With her progressive ideas, and individuality, Lakshmi plays an unparalled role in the Novel.

Sastri represents bourgeois mentality of the contemporary society. Never had he any sympathy for the country, or the Congress or Gandhiji. His sole aim was money, position and fame. He has great admiration for the British Government for the encouragements it gives to people like him. As the Congress movement grows in strength and the political conditions change in its favour, Sastri changes his outward attitudes. In case Congress wins in the freedom struggle, he should not be at a disadvantageous condition. So, he must be in their good books. For this he does not hesitate to court imprisonment. He wears Khadi suit and attends Congress meetings. He observes Hindu religious customs in a conspicuous manner to pose himself as a nationalist. He thus becomes a prominent Congress leader without his selfish pursuits. Opportunists like him had joined the Congress in big numbers in those days and so because of such people the Congress movement received some setback.

There was a period in the National movement when the Nationalists not only eulogised the greatness of our ancient past but also honoured and observed the ancient Hindu customs and traditions. This was done in opposition to western culture and civilisation. In observing their practices, they did not discriminate between the good and the bad of it, but they were carried away emotionally with a feeling that all was good in the past.

It is true this acted as a spur to rouse patriotic feelings. Though this appeared to help the political movement temporarily, it gave a set-back to the society. The great and strenuous work done by our social reformers over the years got eclipsed. The capitalists who received modern education had no faith in these age old customs and practices. But they observed them in accordance with the politics of the National movement of those days, to derive maximum political dividends. The author has exposed their mentality and hypocrisy in this novel. He has analysed this misleading behaviour of the capitalists and this analysis is relevant in today's political conditions also.

Shantham is an honest lady. She has a correct understanding of the contemporary political, economic and social conditions. She is endowed with a progressive social consciousness. It is natural that she is influenced by Gandhiji and the National movement. She wears Khadi, participates in Satyagraha and courts imprisonment. She works in the Harijan uplift movement. She becomes a member of the Congress Working Committee. She is respected by all. She is dissatisfied and disheartened over the attitudes of some of the Congressmen. She grows impatient at her husband's behaviour. In fact, she wants to change his views and attitudes. Though he pretends to change for the sake of Shantham his capitalist mentality does not change.

Shantham who has analysed the social injustices in the capitalist society feels greatly annoyed. On one side there are riches and on the other side there is poverty : While some people roll in dinners, the poor are exposed to utter starvation. Shantham draws Sastri's attention to the glaring inequalities. To this he says "these inequalities and contradictions are not created by me or by you. Class differences like the caste and racial differences exist as part of God's creation? They don't disappear."

This excuse of God's creation is the most powerful weapon employed to deceive the people. Those who never experienced poverty and starvation give such sermons. They want to keep people in ignorance and suppress their capacity to think and gain consciousness. Shantham, who stepped into the outside world, by participating in Sathyagraha and going to jail, has gained experience of life and she easily discerns Sastri's cleverness. She is subjected to great indignities because of Sastri's incorrigible mentality.

All values get collapsed before money in this society. Money occupies the top position. A case of widow's maintenance was under enquiry in a court of law. All social reformers contribute towards the expenses for engaging a lawyer in support of the widow. But Shastri appears on behalf of the proprietor and wins the case. She won't get the maintenance. Shastri receives a huge amount from his client. Shantham feels very bad at this injustice done to a poor widow. Shastri says that he too has sympathy for the poor widow, and he sheds crocodile tears saying that Hindu law is against her. He, accompanied by the press reporters, goes immediately to the Hindu Law Reform Association and donates one thousand rupees. The next day he is elected as its president. This is the contradiction in the capitalist way of life. Sastri makes money knowing full well, that is unjust and immoral. This is the secret of such moral lepers. They get money as well as fame. The chief aim is to earn money by any means. In the novel one sees at every step a presentation of the capitalist mentality and the wretchedness of the social system. The author lays bare in the novel the exploitation of the foreign rulers, as well as our own capitalists resulting in abject poverty of the people.

One day, Shantham sees a poor, pregnant woman searching for crumbs in the dust-bin. This woman was previously employed in the mica mines at Gudur, and due to pregnancy the owners got rid of her. She comes to the city but finds no work.

Shantham too is pregnant, but is able to command all comforts. The poor pregnant lady feels that there is no food to satisfy her hunger. In another case a pregnant woman ends her pregnancy due to lack of food, and even attempts to commit suicide. Sastry appearing on behalf of the prosecution, urges the court to give life sentence to her. Shantham expresses her deep resentment at this grave injustice done to the poor people. She gives leave for one month to her maid servant who is pregnant. Sastri does not like this. He asks sarcastically why money should not be given to her also. "Should we do like this, because it is done so in countries like England and Russia?" If we put into practice such things, and if they know about such facilities and rights, can we secure house maids and servants? Sastri feels deeply worried about this.

Shantham and Sastri, when they visited Pondichery, happened to see a Textile mill and the workers eating amidst machines. They also saw large stocks of the cloth produced by them. But the workers were found wearing rags. Shantham was deeply moved by the things she saw at the Mill. She once dreamed that to eradicate poverty, the country should go in for industrilisation. But now she feels that these machines are running the poor people. She also thinks that because of such evil consequences, Gandhiji has undertaken Khadi movement. Instead of depending upon Mills and filling the coffers of the rich, it would be better to depend upon handlooms.

Shastri with his capitalist mentality, thinks otherwise. He says : The Mill owners with a view to serving the country have invested capital, and given employment to people. Did we ever scold the capitalists as exploiters? It is ingratitude. Shantham wants that the workers should be given shares in industries. Socialist literature, which is useless, is being imported from England. By reading such literature, people like Shantam are getting spoiled.

It is generally said that the poor maintain the rich and not *vice-versa*. Shastri knows full well that it is the labour which fills the coffers of the rich. Nevertheless he feels worried, because of his capitalist mentality. Shastri looks at the children of the workers playing in the gutters and says, "These children do not want to be clean. It is their fate. All our ancient scriptures are of no use to them."

Sastry thus depends on the deceitful karma theory. There is no need for the children of the workers to be dirty if their parents are paid in full for the work they do. If they are under paid thus how can the children of the rich go abroad even at the age of ten? In order to secure all these privileges at the expense of the poor, it is natural for persons like Sastri to defend and propagate capitalistic ideas.

Sastri is always a lawyer for the Zamindars. He defends them in the courts against the farmers. He justifies his action because the farmers cannot pay him such big fees. He justifies it as the ethics of his profession. For the sake of money, he must defend the unjust. But Shantham thinks that one will derive satisfaction if one protects the interests of the farmers. Why not avoid that opportunity? She thinks that C.R. Das by defending the accused in the treason and bomb cases, stood for the people and attained great fame. She desires that Sastri should do the same.

High and low, long and short, rich and poor, feast and fast, joy and sorrow — there is beauty and glamour if these contrasts exist. How can you go against Nature and creation? It will be ludicrous if the scholar and scavenger, servant and cinema star are paid the same salary. God has not bestowed upon us all, equal capacities and status except in the case of myself and my brother and some others. Difference in income is a must. If such people should rise to the top and serve humanity... such people are needed to provide employment to thousands of people. They are needed to give charities and feed the multitude?

This is the trend and tenor of Sastri's thinking. You cannot find army where this kind of cruel and false logic exists. How long can they keep the people ignorant about this false logic and sermons? When the people revolt, they will destroy this system tooth and nail.

In the capitalist system money making plays an important role. "One makes money through insolvency by cheating the creditors, another makes it in the share market. Yet another earns by exploiting the patients. But such persons are respected under this system. The next generation will not know how one becomes rich. He, who does not earn money, is considered inefficient and useless. He will not be respected."

Shantham feels sad that values are linked up with money, which is earned by any means.

"In England in the name of equality women were employed along with men in the mills and they were made slaves by the capitalists. In Russia women are made collective property. Are they human beings or demons?" This is how Sastri goes on commenting on the economic freedom of the women. The capitalists whether they are in England or in any other country, make men and women as their slaves. In the exploitation of labour there is no distinction. A doubt may arise why the capitalist minded Sastri criticizes the capitalists of England. We may mistake that Indian capitalists are kind towards women. But the fact is otherwise.

Sastry is a capitalist with feudal ideas. He fears that if the women become economically free, they may not be under the husbands' dictates and they may revolt if necessary. That is why he thinks that the woman's place is in the house and not outside.

The daughter of Santham's maid servant was a victim of her husband's torture. She tolerates the evil practices of her husband bravely. Shantham questions her why she lives with him inspite of indignities and abuses. How can a helpless woman without any means of livelihood go away from the husband? She will be a burden to any body. So, it is better to put up with him. "How can I love my husband who beats me daily?" Sastri is surprised to hear such things from the daughter of a servant. Sastri cannot realise that life has taught her such things. Every woman today faces the same problem. It is better such women hang themselves says Shantham. She lays much stress on the economic independence of woman.

Woman's freedom and economic independence are not worth discussing according to Sastri. He is embarrassed to hear these words from Shantham. He fears how to cope with his wife who differs form him so much. His marriage with Shantham is a civil marriage and as such there is scope for divorce. "But can a woman avail herself of this right? She cannot avail herself of it for fear of social stigma." Sastri feels thus.

Shantham gives shelter to the destitute girl. Sastri does not like this. He tries to dissuade her by saying that it is better not to bother about such things. Moreover, society may blame them for keeping a grown up girl in their home. Shantham gets enraged at the selfishness of her husband and opposes him. Sastri desperately reconciles to himself by saying that the girl will be atleast useful as a maid servant. He feels that he can make this as a stooge on the next day. "We should utilise every situation profitably. In this only lies one's mettle" Sasthri proves his capitalistic mentality.

It is during the days of Salt Satyagrahs that Santham thinks about politics for the first time seriously. One day she reads "Young India," and Gandhiji makes a special appeal to women on 10th April 1930 to wear khadi. Responding to his appeal, she wears khadi. Sastri does not like her joining Salt Satyagraha. He thinks that it is a mistake to join Satyagraha both economically and politically. He enters politics and prescribes certain qualifications for a politician.

Vast number of people joined the freedom struggle without caring for lives. They did it for the sake of independence and not for the reforms advocated by Gandhiji. The British government used severe repression. The people surged forward, became martyrs and the jails were full. The British government yielded and Gandhi-Irvin pact was concluded. Gandhiji called off the Satyagraha movement. There was not a word about full Independence. When Gandhiji started Dandi March, he assured the people that his movement would not stop till the last Satyagrahi was alive. But why did Gandhiji call off the struggle? There was tantalizing doubt about that.

Inspired by nationalism and Gandhiji's movement many patriotic minded people participated in Satyagraha. Salt Satyagraha is a milestone in the history of freedom movement. But the movement received a set-back due to the British government's policy of Divide and Rule and selfishness of the opportunist politicians and capitalists. Moderates in the Congress do not like the movement to continue. They wanted freedom without making any sacrifice. They were satisfied with dominion status for the country. The Muslims kept themselves aloof from the struggle. The caste differences like Brahmin and Non-Brahmin, scheduled caste and others came to the forefront. On the whole, the movement failed to involve all sections. This was the estimate of Shantham on the movement.

The toiling and moiling of villagers was ignored completely even after the Karachi Congress resolution on socialism. The leadership was passed on into the hands the middle class. Shantham was annoyed about this. People who were in jail only for six months became leaders. If any body criticised them he was doubted either as socialist or communist. The youth felt greatly disappointed and disheartened. They lost respect for the leaders. They had misgivings that the Congress would be dominated by the rich people. They did not like the calling off the Satyagraha struggle by Gandhiji.

The youth who were severely disappointed with the sudden end of the Satyagraha took to secret revolutionary activities. During her trip to Delhi Shantham happened to meet secretly a group of revolutionaries. She noted how those youth who were drawn from highly educated and rich classes were sowing the seeds of revolution. They were exerting day and night to arouse the consciousness of the workers in the Mills and factories.

On the other side, honest Congressmen like Shantham had faith in Gandhiji's leadership and believed that both Swaraj and socialism could be achieved under the leadership of Gandhiji. They earnestly felt that Socialism should be the aim of Swaraj. But after noticing the way electioneering was done in those days they feared that power would pass into the hands of the rich only. Even in the Nineteen Twenties they arose and it had an expression in "Malapalli" a novel written by a powerful Telugu novelist, Unnava Lakshminarayana. Many feared that Swaraj and socialism would be a farce unless the movement of the workers and the oppressed and the depressed, gained momentum.

The fears expressed in those days of the National movement came true 50 years after the Independence as the same political traditional trend is continuing even now. Despite the decades of Independence socialism has remained only as an utopia. In this democracy, politics is dominated by the power mongers of the upper class. Even in the past, there were some who wrote books on socialism, and some others who composed poems on hunger and revolution but they were hypocrites. After her disillusionment with Congress politics Shantham comments thus : "You don't hear the agony of revolution in the Jails — Ashrams are not the places for revolutionary ideas. Their new world is not born in the deliberations of the working committees."

It is the people who must make a revolution and create the Brave New World.

This novel, analyses realistically the nature and essence of the capitalist system and kindles new ideas and awareness in the minds of the leaders. With this object in view, the writer creates the character of Sastri who represents the capitalist society and the character of Shantham who represents the progressive ideals. Shantham exposes and lays bare the selfish nature of capitalism. She brings to light the abject poverty of the working class.

The novel reflects the contemporary ideas and aspirations in a realistic way. The aim of the National Movement should not be only to achieve political independence from foreign rule, but also it should lead to the achievement of socialism and liberation from Swadeshi capitalism. This is the message conveyed in this novel.

In the novel, the reader will come to know the weaknesses of the Independence movement of those days. He will also get a correct understanding of the aims and practices of the present day political movements. The novelist has portrayed the role of Shantham as an ideal lady with deep commitment and understanding. He has shown how the political scene will change with the active role and participation of women. This is as true today as it was in the day of the National Movement.

●

27

Gandhism and Socialism in *Malapalli*

H. S. BRAHMANANDA

Malapalli (1922) a novel by Unnava Lakshminarayana Pantulu (1873-1958) is regarded as a herald of the progress of the depressed classes, symbolised in the character of Ramadas, a Harijan who rose to the heights of the 'Mahatma' in his spiritual and social image. The novel was also called 'Sangavijayam' (the victory of society) otherwise symbolised in the character of Sangadas, the son of Ramadas.

The period between 1920 and 1947 has been called the 'Gandhian era of Independence struggle'. It was in this period that the novel was written. Unnava by appearance was very much a Gandhian : but he was an activist inspired by the 'socialist' concept of revolution. He was instrumental in leading the grass Satyagraha (Pullar Poratam) of Palnadu, for which he was jailed at Rayavellore. There he was associated with the great leaders like Madabhushi, Gampalagudem Maharaja and social workers like Vennelakanti Raghavaiah and Desireddy Seshareddy.

Everyday after finishing a portion of the novel, Unnava used to read it for his colleagues and his friends used to prepare a duplicate of it on the same day. One of the copies was sent out, thanks to the sympathetic jail wardens, and thus the novel was brought out in parts. The other copy owned by Unnava was confiscated by the British Government.

Malapalli is a very big novel running into about one thousand pages with divergent ideas and innumerable characters. Its concern was that though 'Gandhism' was the royal way of Indian independence struggle, some constitutional changes must be made before India became Independent. Probably the novelist had in his mind that a sort of 'Socialist Democracy' should be achieved once independence was granted to India. The theme and its execution has proved that he has great regard for Gandhian concept of 'Satyagraha' and at the same time he has his own appreciation of socialist revolution of Russia, though with a few reservations of his own.

But it is an astonishing fact that the novel was banned by the then British Government due to pressure from the members of the Justice party, who protested that the novel contained undesirable comments on one section of the upper class non-Brahmins. But a careful reading of the novel reveals that Unnava was not against any caste, but in his understanding the ultimate aim of the struggle was to be 'social change' and not merely a 'political transition' of the power from the British to the Indians.

The Novel is divided into 4 parts :

(1) Ramdas and his family Venkatadas, Sangadas, Malakshmi, Jyoti, Rangadu live happily in the Village 'Mangala Puram'. The chief of the Village Chowdaraiah does not like his son Ramanayudu, sympathising and mixing with Sangadas, the son of Ramadas, who is interested in the progress of Harijans. A State level meeting is organised by Sangadas. Chowdaraiah dislikes all these and beats Sangadas with an iron rod. Sangadas dies.

(2) Sanga Peetham is established in the name of Sangadas. Kamalamma, the wife of Ramanaidu elopes with one of the relatives, a young man by name Mohan Rao. They go to Madras. Kamalamma gives birth to a boy and she is attacked by plague. Mohan Rao finds his own match and marries. Chowdaraiah goes on teasing Ramadas on various grounds. Venkatadas leaves the house and becomes 'Takkella Jaggadu' and terrorises the government.

(3) Ramadas and his family are kept in the settlement meant for thieves and dacoits. The Christian Father and Mr. Paul, a converted Christian cause many difficulties to the family of Ramadas. Ramadas and Malakshmi are also jailed. Jyoti, in order to escape molestation at the hands

of Paul, falls into the river Krishna and passes away. Appadas, the nephew of Ramadas, who is in love with Jyothi, also ends his life along with Jyoti. Jaggadu is captured and jailed. He is sent to central jail, where Ramadas and Malakshmi have already been put.

(4) The life in jail is horrible. Ramadas and Pullappa are stripped off their clothes. Their heads are shaven completely. Ramadas takes it as the starting point of his future 'Ashram' of 'Sanyasa'. He meets his son Venkatadas (Jaggadu) and appreciates his work, though he is not ready to accept his path 'totally' as good. Malakshmi and Jaggadu too pass away. Ramadas is found 'least' disturbed, by all these happenings. He stands still like a 'yogi'. He earns for himself in the jail by working on 'Charkha' and doing labour along with other inmates. With the declaration of independence, the prisoners are released. Ramadas is taken in procession to his village. Venkataiah and Ramanaidu establish two colleges, one for the labourers and the other for the depressed classes. Ramadas is made its principal. He practises 'YOGA' and leaves the world in 'Meditation'. Parts 1 to 3 were alone published first. The 4th part was published with great difficulty in 1935-36 by Nageswara Rao Panthulu, the 'Doyen' of Telugu journalism.

From the life sketch available to us, we understand that Unnava was sent to Ireland for his education. There he met Irish leaders like De Vera and was very much impressed by the on going Russian Revolution in general and 'Bolshevik' movement in particular.

Reflecting Unnava's background, Vankata Reddy, the president of the Sangh in his address at the state level meeting of Harijan Day says as follows :

"You might have heard of Sangadasu,"

our own leader. Though he belongs to our own community of Harijans, he is concerned about the overall development of Hindu community. His interest is not a narrow one. He firmly believes that the progress of the nation is of primary importance on which depends the growth of communities. The old traditions of all the countries have proved ineffective in the modern times. Same is the case with India. In France and America, the princely class and the clergy have been destroyed and the people's government has appeared, but the power is still concentrated in the hands of the aristocrats who are minor in strength. Because of this, the poor and the oppressed who are in majority found themselves in great troubles. Hence, the 'working section' and the 'oppressed' have come forward to change the situation. In Italy the capitalists and the labourers have entered into an agreement, consequent to the confiscation of industry by the labourers. In Russia Soviet government has come into power. This is called Bolshevism, which means 'the opinion of the majority'.

Speaking at length about Bolshevism and Leninism, the president says : "The influence of Bolshevism is there on the British intelligentsia. But the State does not want to encourage even the thought of Bolshevism. The women are given the right to vote. It is certain that under the new electorate, the number of working class is certain to increase. And we don't yet know, how it is going to change the government in England and thereby in India "(181-182).

We are astonished to find that, this is what exactly happened in these two countries afterwards. The following statement by the writer about the social reconstruction in India is very crucial in the context of the 'Class struggle' which has been a neglected aspect. The writer says :

"In our country the labourers have no right to vote. Of all the countries it is in India that the society requires a total reconstruction. In the other countries also we find labourers being poor, but not in crores, without food shelter as we find in our country. As a result of the division of castes on the basis of occupations, the money has been concentrated only at the hands of landlords and businessmen. A few people say that we should reject the 'Varnadharma' — but we should remember that if the 'occupations' are gone, what do they do and how will they live? So we should not follow the revolutionary methods right now. Let us follow the British method. Will the landlords lose their lands and distribute them to the poor! Is it justifiable on our part to demand so? They should also follow 'Dharma' and give the labourers their due. The lands in the forest and Banjar areas have to be allotted to them. But the immediate responsibility of the 'rich' is to impart education to the 'downtrodden'. They should no more neglect this. Our movement is a sacred one. There is no room for hatred (enmity) in our pious path. A movement with hatred as its main inspiration cannot stand by itself. Let us not hate each other. Let the non-Harijans help our movement. Let us accept the change. Change is the symbol of awareness, and rigidity is a symbol of death.

The entire novel is an explanation of these lines. While the actions of Ramadas and Sangadas symbolise Gandhian ideas of non-violence and peaceful co-existence, the other characters soon realise the pathetic results of Gandhism. They suffer a lot, but yet do not deviate from their path of non-violence. The elder brother of Sangadas, by name Venkatadas refuses to follow his father any more and leaves the village. He chooses 'Dharma Kannam operation', by which he loots the rich and feeds the helpless and protects the distressed women. He terrorises the state in the name of one 'Takkella Jaggadu' who had passed away a few years before, as per the police records.

While Chowdaraiah goes on intimidating and cornering the family of Ramadas and finally confiscates his property, Ramadas is rendered helpless. He chooses to go for business of Textile on commission basis. The men of Jaggadu take away the clothes and give Ramadas 400 rupees, double the rate expected from Subbisetty.

The men sing as follows :

"Rama Rama Sri Rama Rama Rama Raghurama!"

Keep in mind the teaching of Takkella Jaggadu. In the ancient times all were brothers and sisters. The property was everybody's — no rich no poor, with the onset of Kaliyuga the picture altered, the rich became richer — the poor the poorer. The labourer is bonded to the rich. No way to come out as such.

O workers! if you all unite
The world is yours! build your mite
Under guilds and prove your strength
Do not fight nor abuse — you reach your goal
Non cooperation is the only way — no other way
'Equality' is our aim — the 'Krita'
Will be brought again! (2-53-55)

After the hand and leg of Jaggadu are cut off, he lies helpless in the Central jail of Nidadavolu. While nearing the point of death, he refuses to pronounce the name of Rama, and argues thus :

> "Rama... he might be a god, but not a kind hearted one. He has made the entire world a city of all sins. If 'He' is there at all, it is high time that all the people attacked him and brought him onto the right path" (obviously 'humanity').

At the end of the conversation with his father, he asks him how he took his activity of 'Dharma Kannam'. Ramadas replies :

> "Your drama is a perfectly new one. The rules are your own. You have cut a new path, which I followed the ordinary way along with others. I do not complain that your path is wrong; but one should wait and see how it goes if all people follow it. Your method is legally sound. But I am afraid that there is 'risk' in it, and a difficult method for every one to follow."

He also says :

> "I don't have commitment to 'Dharma' as you have. What is the use of mere solutions? One should purify one's own soul" (2-284-286).

Here lies the real spirit of Unnava's creative mind. While he picturises Ramadas as an embodiment of Sanathana Dharma, he is not against Socialist thought.

But yet, he does not believe in the leftist method of totally changing the economic foundations of the society. To him Jaggadu was a good Samaritan, not a revolutionary. His Dharmakannam (Digging a hole in the Wall) operation was not a dacoity, but a 'Dharma' to achieve social equality. To him 'Caste' is no criterion to judge one's own merit. But yet he was not an 'atheist', but a follower of 'Achalayoga' and Ramanuja's thought of 'equality' of men before God as interpreted by Pilla Lokacharya and Manavula Mahamuni.

Towards the end of the novel, Ramadas sums up as follows :

> If this Brahminism creates the feeling that I am a superior, it should be left off. But the high caste is a natural reason for 'pride' and 'prejudice' and so they are far removed from God; which for the lower castes, it is the opposite. For high castes, the pride comes with the birth. 'Humility' comes with the birth of the outcastes. And so the puranas

say that the Rishis used to stand at the door steps of Dharmavyadha for getting their doubts clarified. And so many Indian brothers! Leave off your prejudice and join hands with our Harijan brothers. Our unity is sure to benefit both the sections" (2-356).

Sangadas described the hunger of Harijans as follows :

"Sirs! If you have ears do listen to me. In our Harijan hamlets full meals for four months means 'maize rice' and Gongura Karam' (curry of Goru leaves). The remaining four months 'half meal', and the rest of four months thorough fasting" (2-105).

Sangadas is a theist due to the teachings of his father. One day, he observes, how the merchant woman cheats and chides the Harijan woman during business. On seeing these, Sangadas fears whether "he would also become an atheist." Unnava's mind seems to dwindle between 'Non-violence' and 'revolution'! He calls the former the 'Dharmapath' and the latter one the 'heroic path'. While he personally favours the former, he rightfully accepts the fact that the common people are favouring the revolutionary path, which is easy for them to understand and execute. Thus, Unnava seems to have visualised that revolutions are brought about by masses, and not by a few individuals, or intellectuals.

But true to his name Ramadas, remained as a 'Karmayogi' and led a relentless war not against the rich or the cruel, but against his own self which was occupied by the six internal enemies (Arishat Varga). At the end, as Pullappa puts it rightly about Ramadas :

Both his head and thoughts were shaven off and is now fit to attain oneness with the 'Brahmman'. Now, he is no more a 'Samsari' but a perfect 'Yati'.

By this description of Ramadas, the novel assumes the depth of an 'epic' like Mahabharata in which the external format of the socio-political story is interrelated to the internal format of man becoming a superman, by becoming 'free' from illusion and bondage! Thus, *Malapalli* stands as an original writing by a Telugu novelist, to depict Indian national movement from the Harijan point of view.

A lot of Russian literature seems to have appeared in Telugu by 1922. Krovvidi Linga Raju's, '*Amma*' (*Mother* of Gorky) was published in 1921. Tapi Dharma Rao had brought into Telugu

Tolstoy's '*Anna Karenina*' Rentala Gopalakrishna and Bellamkonda Ramdas had translated Tolstoy's 'War and Peace' as '*Samaram-Santi*, and many other Russian and Finnish writings were brought into Telugu. Some critics say that Unnava might have been influenced by Henry Woods' '*East line*' to attempt *Malapalli*. But there is no doubt that *Malapalli* is an original Indian Novel, and Unnava was rightly called the Andhra Gorky.

Finally, it is to be remembered that as early as 1913, Tallapraggada Suryanarayana in his '*Helavathi*' and Venkata Parvatheesa Kavulu in '*Mathrumandiram*' (1918) had taken notice of the plight of Harijans, even before Gandhiji started Harijan movement.

Probably 'Brahma Samaj' is the main source of influence on these writings including Unnava to look at Harijans from the point of equality. For the Brahma Samajists, the motto is 'Brahmaiva Kevalam' (The Brahman is Unique and undifferentiated) Unnava was true to himself in accepting 'Gandhism' and socialism from his own perception of Brahman, where the spirit and action are correlated with 'Wisdom'.

Ramadas says :

> "The creation is not a myth, nor an illusion. It is a field of work (Karmakshetra) intended to improve your positive qualities."

It is a fitting tribute to what Unnava did for the Indian society by way of his own writing.

●

28

Guilt and Atonement — Mukul Kesavan's *Looking Through Glass*

BABLI GUPTA

It is suggested that the novel be read as creative text of subaltern history. The subaltern approach sets its agenda by contesting the notion that in societies fragmented by class, race, religion, ethnicity and gender there can be a single, completely objective viewpoint giving history in totality, highlighting the need therefore to chronicle the narratives of those who are silenced by dominant hegemonic groups. The debate in this case centres on the Congress' version of the Quit India Movement and the versions of those who disagreed with it. Kesavan reconstructs the contesting voices by taking himself, as unconcealed narrator, across the time-wrap to enter India of 1942, while retaining the memory of the present, constantly measuring events of the past and their effect upon the future.

The narrator, a whimsical anti-hero, is embroiled in his grandmother's guilt, arising from her failure to participate in the Quit India Movement at Gandhi's call, thus reducing her status from a share-holder to a debtor of the Indian Republic. For Dadi, a staunch Gandhian, had been taught to believe in the Congress agit prop that all those who failed to participate in the movement had forfeited their right to earn a place in history. Henceforth, defaulters ranging from the Muslim League to the Communists and lapsed Gandhians like Dadi herself, were put outside the pale of freedom movement — traitors perhaps, "There was no room for feeble nuances in 1942."[1]

This theatricalized displacement gives the grandchild a chance to participate in the re-run of events and undo Dadi's wrongs. This opportunity is deliberately set aside and an oppositional viewpoint to the history of 1942 is inserted in its place. The narrator finds an alternative perspective to history by sharing the life of Masroor and his family. He comes to share their viewpoint and anxieties about the outcome of this hastily engineered call and its adverse impact on Hindu-Muslim relations fast deteriorating in climate of mutual suspicion with communal riot closing in upon their cherished Lucknow, "Only six months ago Gandhi himself had said that he wouldn't start a Civil Disobedience movement without a settlement of the Hindu-Muslim question. But now, said Masroor agitatedly... he is asking us to do or die. If they go ahead with this Quit India business, he said more quietly, Jinnah will have his Pakistan by the end of the decade" (LTG 38).

Congress' mismanagement ensures the success of Muslim league, conceived as an ideological counter-weight to secular Nationalism. Together they are held responsible for vivisecting what is more than the geographical boundaries of India. They overthrow a way of life, uproot a whole tradition of blended culture and rob the newly minted nation of their shared history. Masroor's family is mounted as a perfect vehicle of this tradition threatened with eminent destruction.

Masroor's mother Begum Kulsum Ganjoo, scion of Syed family, marries a Kashmiri Brahmin, Charandass Ganjoo converted to Islam for his love of Urdu and the lady, in that order. (Urdu is considered a language of high literary refinement, written in Perso-Arabic script and spoken chiefly in India). The Begum devotes her one woman journal Khatoon in Urdu for re-inventing separate life for women outside their homes, "Till women reinvent the world, she said to me, who will let them live in it?" (LTG 18). Masroor her son, is a man who would be Nehru. Like his counterpart from the future, he too is burdened with ancestral guilt. His grandfather had aspired "To merge the destiny of the Ganjoos with Indian Nationalism" (LTG 30). Unlike his grandfather, Masroor does not view his parent's conversion to Islam as a serious impediment in fulfilling his ambition to be a nationalist leader with Nehru as a surrogate father. That is, before the Congress' betrayal which practically strips the Muslim leaders within Congress of their identity and role. They are the first victims in the Nehru-Jinnah tussle to gain exclusive control over the Muslim masses.

Nehru and Jinnah — opponents on the political chessboard, exist as mutually bound contenders. Nehru plays with the advantage of the white pawns. Projected as the undisputed leader of the Congress and therefore India, he is poised to inherit the highest office of the land as ancestral right. Aristocratic privileging is augmented with a progressive profile as Nehru plays out the Marxist idea of the "historical agent" pre-destined to fulfil this historical role. Quite naturally he blunders from over-confidence.

The Congress brushes aside all reservations about the manner and timing of the call for Quit India. They overlooked Gandhi's solemn promise to the Muslims as well as the importunations of the Muslim Congressmen, who were caught in the crossfire between threatened ostracism by the Muslim League and the Congress Party's lack of confidence in their sincerity when they pleaded for more time to bring around the Muslim masses to Congress's point of view. The party instead, conjures a glib formula of mathematically subtracting the numerical strength of the Muslims from the total population to reach the conclusion that they no longer needed the Muslims for their purpose :

> "Like a bunch of Yogis fired by the power of the mind, they concentrated on the Hindu-Muslim problem, and made it vanish. Along with the problem, said Masroor, we vanished as well" (LTG 247).

With brittle wit and mordant humour Kesavan sketches the magical disappearance of the Muslim misfits to underscore the crux of the matter. That, by squeezing out of space the likes of Masroor-activist, artist, poet, journalist and intellectual who truly believed in the secular credentials of the Congress Party and who could have acted as a bridge between the two communities, Congress blundered monumentally. The fear-ridden community left with no other leadership is driven straight towards the Muslim League, with Jinnah, knight of the black Pawns, waiting in the wings to make his moves.

The author handles the Jinnah factor, with sympathetic understanding tinged with regret :

> "It had been a long road for him, from the Parsi Bombay and the Hindu-Muslim advocacy of his early years, to the

> Quid-Ship and the demand for Pakistan, and he must have had his reasons" (LTG 177).

He does not endorse his viewpoint for that reason. Nehru saw himself at least, as an agent of change. Jinnah in counter-move treats, "History not as a live agent, but a dead record which supplies precedence for his great political brief" (LTG 315). He succeeds in dragging history backwards to carve out a purified nation-Pakistan, cleansed of its earlier blemish of mixed origin and shared culture. The irony of, "An Islamic State founded by a pork-eating barrister," (LTG 177) is not lost upon the founder who justifies himself as prisoner of time. When asked if he really desired partition of India, he wrote, "Barristers do not have opinions — they have briefs" (LTG 177).

Jinnah's fatalism infects the author. Curiously, a book designed to explore alternative choices in history whittles down the actual choice to little more than a Gandhi, Jinnah, Nehru discourse. A different history, as found in the struggle of peasants, workers, subalterns of the army, dalits, women and other marginalised segments is glossed over or treated within an unaccountable degree of cynical pessimism. For example, the Mappila revolt where the Muslim peasantry had struggled for decades against predominantly Hindu landlords, finds mention only to note the counter-reactionary wave of Hindu revivalism which finds place in Kerala's history for the first time in the period when the movement begins to decline. The Hindu zealots instigated by the landlords engineer the bogey of forced conversion, while actually conspiring to crush the predominantly Muslim peasantry. In the process, Haasan is mistaken for a Muslim looking for converts and captured by the enraged mob. In consequence, "A Middle-aged Hindu from Mysore [is] branded like a cow" (LTG 71). The sweeping tide of the Khilafat Movement where Gandhi had succeeded in making the Hindus and Muslims fight the Imperialists instead of each other is mentioned in passing, once again, as a movement on the wane. A book, concerned sincerely with the prospects of communal amity as an alternative to the disaster of partition, could surely have found more by way of precedence and positive response here than anywhere else!

Most significantly, the attitude to the problematized period of 1942 is symptomatic of a general predisposition. On his way to

Banaras to immerse his grandmother's ashes in the Ganga, the Storyteller is taken captive by the victorious insurrectionists of Azamgarh and forcibly made to witness the attack on Mudhuban, at a time when mass insurgencies had swept over Uttar Pradesh giving a severe jolt to British rule. Here the incident becomes an occasion which is trivialized into a comic farce. A time for recording, and ridiculing the sexual fantasies of comrade 'ratface' towards a comely woman leader, ending the recital on a fairly complacent note recording the woman's death as well as the near certainty of the death of the movement.

With all its shortcomings was the period when mass insurgencies — however sporadic and disorganized had succeeded in putting, for a while, the Raj on the run, draining its vigour in the remaining years of its stay. The authorial response, always alert to the retreat of such popular movements is regretfully myopic in assessing the period of their advance which must precede the retreat in the first place. Ironically then, we end up with an undervaluation of people's struggle which is not unlike one-sidedness found in official versions of history.

To say this is not to take away from the merit of the attempt to demystify carefully constructed myths. It is only an acknowledgment of certain gray areas which creep into all methodologies, including the author's, as well as this critic's in their use of analytical tools for investigating their world so that, we may not end up with one set of fallacies replacing the other! The attempt here is to understand the 'mind-set' of the author and the roots of his cynicised pessimism which is revealed most tellingly in the way he constructs the career and ultimate destiny of Chaubey — student leader, failed revolutionary, central actor of mythological drama and blue film ending his career as human canon ball in a circus, licking his wounds.

As captain of the Banaras Hindu University Cricket team Chaubey is as determined as Masroor to prevent a friendly match with the Aligarh Muslim University cricket team for opposite reasons. He will not be satisfied with the mini-war which the match promises to become, choosing instead to lead his team to join the rebels at Azamgarh with a more exalted scheme in mind. He would like to use the period of mass insurrection as a dress-rehearsal for the ultimate war to be waged for the revival of the lost glory of the Hindu Kingdom as found in the reign of king Vikramaditya. Abandoning the revolt after its defeat he turns towards Banaras, the site of Hindu revivalism. Here, he bends his energies to serve Pandit Pant Ram the wrestler who runs an 'akhara' and dreams to stage the revised Ramayana as a modern political allegory with a tail-less muscularized Hanuman occupying centre-stage, instead of Ram. The anxieties of our present are being read into events of the past with the focus on the demolition of Babari Masjid by frenzied mob who claim to be the modern-day worshippers of Hanuman determined to realize Pandit Pant Ram's dream at last. The distress and pessimism that permeates the author's vision comes from this unwritten fear about the dangerous outcome of the failed revolutions past and present. Because of the counterproductive reaction and irrational violence which comes to the surface when dreams turn sour. This perhaps produces the timorous response in the author towards popular modes of struggle in history.

The cult of disbelief answers for the personal weakness. It is indicative of the outlook found in most post-colonial thinkers and writers, who have as yet to distinguish between the necessity of rational scepticism and the need to deconstruct an uncritically imbibed faith from the imperative to place their belief in some positive frame of reference, inspite of the risk of facing disillusionment. What is needed is resilience to failure, a quality which the author already possesses. For the book has a remarkably resilient quality which sets it apart from the run-of-the-mill post-modernist fiction steeped in self-indulgent pessimism and flight from reality.

The recovery from this mood of complete defeat in this book is because of the narrator's sincere involvement with other human beings. At the heart of the novel is the commitment to those idealized figures who become his family and friends in the 'alien times'. For whose sake he removes the glass separating them from him in time and dissolves himself in history.

The focal point is given in Ammi's resistance to mindless change. Like Gandhi whose vision was growlingly at variance with Congress, Ammi makes a retreat from politics when she finds that her purpose is greatly misunderstood. As a Muslim lady she is expected to permanently wear the veil, support the cause of Pakistan and cheerfully join the exodus. Whereas for Ammi, "Anjuman Bara-I-Tahaffuz-I-Hall," is not a Muslim party. It is a society for the "defence of the present" (LTG 333). Her gameplan, a curious mix of childish trivia and astute wisdom, reminiscent of Gandhian thought[2], cautions fellow countrymen to preserve what they can of their blended past instead of carving out two antagonistic nations, purged of each others presence through sword and bloodshed. Preservation of Lucknow used as an extended metaphour is the object of Bukhey, Bihari, and Jamal Mian's daily supplication to Baba Farid with renderings of the Quranic Verse into hot fried sweets The Jalebis were supposed to save Lucknow from going the Kanpur way, which had been licked by communal fires already, because Bihari had not kept the word on a single day. The narrator's gusty participation in these enterprises, foreclosed to doom would slide into sentimentalism but for the sustained comedy and the pose of the funny man which masks the gravity of his final choice, made in the footsteps of Haasan.

Haasan, mistaken by all for a Shia Muslim, a permanent fixture in Masroor and Ammi's household is in fact — H.Y. Narasimhamurthy, Iyengar Brahmin who mistaken and branded for being a Muslim, voluntarily assumes that identity in order to rid himself of all signs of identification through religion. His ethical code while talking of generalities "love for all essential humanity, unclassified, unclothed," places his commitment firmly with those who are weak and victimized, to share their fears and fortunes. Haasan in one of his disguises shares the name Kesavan with the author. The author, as narrator re-enacts Haasan's moral choice in the concluding movement of the book. He takes care all the while to conceal his absolute earnestness under the cover of a rollicking farce where the brown waiter, as narrator becomes the object of a white woman's lust. On the pretext of consummating the union thwarted for the flimsiest reason, he accomplishes his real intention, inflicting upon himself the wound of circumcision to become a member of the marked race :

> "... circumcised monsters who bathe once a year and breed all the time" (LTG 189).

Partition has become the metaphor of estrangement. The process by which people separate themselves from each other, permanently alien and hostile forever. The embattled legacy of our past finds so many ways of spilling into our present and sets the imperative to understand how history shapes our present. Not wholly or determinatively because it offers us so many histories instead of one. Leaving room to elect a perspective and adopt a course of action expressing one's choice. The voluntary self-exile of the protagonist at the end when he, alongwith Haasan joins the Muslim refugees at the camp set at Purana Quila, is a weak symbiotic expiation of guilt. It recalls to mind the Gandhian approach both in its inadequacies as well as its merits. The choice for example Gandhi made, also symbolically, of staying away at Noakhali in the former East Bengal with the riots victims instead of sharing the hour of victory with the riot victims instead of sharing the hour of victory with Nehru at Red Fort, when Freedom came at midnight with Partition as its price-tag.

The limitations of Gandhian thought are made painfully explicit. Inspite of all that, the presence of Gandhi continues to haunt the conscience of the nation. What is not easy to ignore is the Gandhian attitudinal response to issues of ethics and morality. The obstinate insistence of dragging centre-stage, questions of morality in a political debate, most often to the discomfort of all. The single achievement of Mukul Kesavan's first novel is this refreshing and well timed return to considerations of ethical morality in art. The attempt to link the choice of ethics with the choice of perspective in the study of life and history, spiced with wit and humour and mellowed with touching sincerity. This holds the promise that it may still be possible to write novels with a social purpose in this age of disbelief and return to art some of its attributes of purposeful social activity.

NOTES

1. Henceforth all references to the text are in parenthesis (LTG) with pagination.
2. Maulana Abul Kalam Azad, *India Wins Freedom* (the complete version), Orient Longman, 1989. Azad infers that Gandhi was not categorical about launching the movement at that time : "He also was studying the situation and he still believed that a way out may be found" (p. 85). At the same time he was baffled and irritated when immediately after their arrest Gandhi asked him to, "fight on a minor issue like the extension of certain personal facilities to me" (p. 89).

29

A Modern Pilgrim's Progress : Kasthuri Sreenivasan's *The Light From Heaven*

S. KRISHNA SARMA

The Light From Heaven (1990) by Kasthuri Sreenivasan is a disturbing book. In its brief span, the novel is an earnest attempt to project the problem of caste in South Indian society. It is an individual's penance to offset the social malaise, an endeavour to transcend the system. As can be anticipated it is a social tragedy.

Balasubrahmanyam, or Balan is the son of Mr. Seshadri Iyer, a clerk in the Collector's Office at Kamalapur. His twenty nine year old sister is still unmarried because of the basic poverty of Mr. Iyer and of the added congenital limp. Balan was initiated into Brahminhood in his twelfth year, because it was the thing to be done, not because his father could afford it. Through his readings of the classics and observation of things around, Balan becomes acutely aware of the hypocrisy surrounding him and the ritualridden complacency and blind observance of tradition among his community. His mother is a fundamentalist and his father a middle class traditionalist lacking in initiative. He could not get admission into Medical College because of his caste. Even after graduation he fails to get a job because of the communal stigma. When his sister would not marry her boss the widowed Mr. Kandaswamy, because she could not defy the social code, Balan's frustration turns sour; he sees the entire community suffering from a spiritual limp. His situation indicates not merely a social malaise, but a communal guilt, not an oppression as a result of unhealthy social stratification, so much as a punishment for the age-old tyranny perpetrated by his caste on others — the sins of the fathers visiting on the children. Balan rebels — not against the society which refuses to duly reward his merit, but — against his own community which had for three thousand years oppressed the others, treated them like scum, dirt under thin feet, like untouchables not to be recognised or countenanced.

He feels oppressed by the generations' tyranny and hypocrisy. By discarding his sacred thread and letting it drift on the currents of the river, he hopes to renounce his brahminhood; but ironically, he accompanies the act with chanting a few made-up mantras : the ritualism had been imbued in him deeply. Gradually it grows upon him that he should apologise to the world for the sins of the community, bear the sins on himself and to atone for them. And the only way to atone for the sins not his own seems to be to become an untouchable — the lowest of the lowly. In the face of solid disapproval from his family he leaves home.

He wanders from place to place in search of work, but he is doubly handicapped; his education and caste-upbringing are too obvious for him to pass off as a commoner, and his unaccustomed-to-hard-work hands are not a recommendation for hard labour. He seeks to roughen his hands by working on hands and knees. Like some pilgrims he had noticed when the hands get calloused and start bleeding, he starts crawling on elbows-taking the entire thing on a part of penance. Exhausted through strain, exposure and lack of food, he faints on the road and is rescued, fended and fed by an untouchable woman. The Chakkiliyan Pappa and her husband Kuppan of Sirumudi village take him into their house, only after getting the full details about Balan's past and his penance. Kuppan wonders, "I wouldn't want to be a Brahmin, even if I could. We are born, each one of us, to a particular station in life and we want to accept it. So, I can't understand why he wants to be an untouchable" (p. 51). Yet he permits him to stay on and assists him in his work; Balan too welcomes the opportunity so he could absorb the untouchable way of life.

If covering up his literacy and sophisticasion threaten to expose him, it proves much more difficult for him to tolerate the stench of the curing leather in which Kuppan deals. As a 'good' Chakkiliyan, Balan should have to learn the trade. And still more difficult is the revulsion he felt to eating meat. It is with a tremendous will power that he could overcome the revulsion, taking the whole thing as a stage in his penance on his way to becoming an untouchable. He picks up the essentials of the chakkiliyan way of life-eating, drinking and thinking — enough to pass muster, and to assist Kuppan in sandal making. He even introduces some new fashions and attracts the more sophisticated clientele, and does make money, and proves to be quite popular. Since his goal is to become a scavenger, he could not stay on at Sirumudi but had to move. He announces to Kuppan that he wished to go to a small town to try to become a scavenger. Though Kuppan and Pappa feel that Balan was proving to be ungrateful, they realise the drive in him pushing him forward, and so permit him to go.

He goes to Kallupatti a town not too big in which he would have got lost nor too small as would make him conspicuous. There he falls in with Chennan, Lachi and their family to whom he gives out that he was a chakkiliyan brought up by his uncle at Sirumudi, and that he had come over to try to become a scavenger. Pichu and Murugan, Chennan's friends, are surprised that one who knows sandal making should want to clean others filth. Till he could find employment, he sets up a sandal-repairing stall. The sanitary Inspector who comes to object to this is nullified with a free repair of his sandals, and thereafter he is left in peace.

Balan had experienced occasional hallucinations while chatting with his friend Ganesh at Kamalapur; this had slowly developed into frequent meditations while Balan was at Sirumudi : he saw the difference between prayer and meditation — "prayer was addressing god for a specific purpose, usually a selfish one... But meditation was undertaken for self-purification..." (90), it left him "purer and better" (91); and the same comes in handy when he has to use the stinking latrine in the scavenger's colony. His amicability, soft-spokenness and work-mindedness win him friends, he gets a small job in a rich man's house, mainly with the help of Lachi — and finally even the job of a scavenger in the Municipality this, through the machinations of Pichu. Again it is Pichu's slanderous insinuations which precipitate the wedding of Balan and Lachi. Married to the untouchable Lachi, and himself employed as scavenger, Balan feels fulfilled — feels that he had achieved his goal of total conversion to untouchability. "It was as if his vow had been fulfilled, as if his long, hard journey was at and end" — as if he had finally arrived.

But two problems crop up. First, the meditation of Balan, which Lachi had noticed with trepidation, grows on him more and more frequent, occasionally leaving him into a trance, as if his spirit had separated from his body. The folks of the colony come to know of this, and in their naivety, see in it some kind of godliness; attributing divine powers, they flock round him. Especially the women folk seek blessings from him for their children. Secondly, an article appears in a local news paper about a Brahmin youth taking to scavenging. Pichy, who had always been suspicious of Balan, smells a rat, and rushing to Sirumudi and hence to Kamalapur, he investigates into the antecedents of Balan. He returns gleefully and seeks to explode the Balan myth and to expose him. But the latter is unperturbed and owns up the truth — explaining to the distraught Chennan and Lachi why he had to undertake a penance and how he had emerged a complete untouchable and why he had to keep it a secret till that moment.

The truth spreads like wild fire and all folks — the Municipal authorities who had employed him as a scavenger, the upper caste people who were angry with him or sorry for him or sympathetic to his penance, and the media persons who try to sell the hot news — all react sharply to the exposure. Balan could not be dismissed as he had not got the job under false pretences, the public could not do anything to avoid the embarrassment as Balan refuses all help, and the media persons go away in appreciation as he gives them a simple, straight and logical explanation for his actions, rounding it off with his philosophy of the "brotherhood of man and the fatherhood of god" (p. 144). Pichu's efforts to launch a strike demanding Balan's dismissal find no response, and the meeting called to blacken Balan backfires because the latter, in his inimitable simple style, explains how he has become a true chakkiliyan not through mere conversion but through total identification — eating and drinking like them, worshipping their gods, and by doing their work. Pichu grows desperate and in frustration attacks Balan in an ambush and stabs him.

His friend Ganesh who had been responsible for exposing Balan — with all good intensions though — arrives and gets the best medical attention possible for his friend. Seshadri Iyer and Lakshmi come seeking reconciliation. But two days later Balan dies, leaving a distraught Lachi in the cave of Ganesh. He is cremated at the place where he had started as a sandal maker; and in the open space near by they build platform with a statue of Balayogi — a temple symbolising Balan's belief in the brotherhood of men.

The novel has a single focus : it relentlessly presents a modern pilgrim's progress, starting into the protest, renunciation and rebellion, moving on to imitation and apprenticeship, leading through the valley of Shadow of Doubt and Revulsion to the final realisation of the goal, a fulfilment. The struggle undertaken by the protagonist is too gigantic, the powers he fights are too deep-rooted and too widely spread in the society, for a single individual to be able to uproot or vanish them. Given the scenario, it appears inevitable that he should be eliminated for, as long as incompetent and feckless Seshadri Iyers and orthodox fundamentalists on the one hand, and jealous and evil minded Pichus on the other people in the society, it is impossible for a Balan to survive.

Moreover, the writer has woven a certain tragic inevitability into the texture of the plot : obduracy rather than 'hubris' may be the flaw in Balan's character and Pichu's world is threatened by his arrival on the scene, and the contrarious forces which would ultimately overwhelm Balan are let loose even on the day he set foot in Kallupatti. And Pichu constitutes a sort of evil genius for Balan, aiming to work against his interest. That is how Balan is offered the job of cleaning the colony latrine, that is how he is pushed into his wedding with Lachi — which anyway both of them desired — and again that is how his final betrayal is brought about. And, in a cathartic fashion, the quintessence of "Balanism" gets established through the efforts of Ganesh and Lachi. Maybe Balan's "Sanctification" required that he should die "when a Brahmin becomes a scavenger voluntarily", says Ganesh at the end, "the next step, obviously has to be divinity. There is no room for him in this world" (p. 161). The novel in no way could have ended on a comic note : Balan is not cast in such a mould, for one thing, and in addition the focus of the thrust would have been dissipated and the point blunted.

However, the title of the novel in misleading. What is this 'Light from Heaven' doing in the context of a social de-stratification and of a spiritual progress of the protagonist was sainthood implied in the title? This does not appear to be reasonable.

Probably the title was chosen as an afterthought — and a rather pretentious one, at that. In addition there are two obvious flaws in the novel which distract and confuse the reader. One is the poetic description of the river with which the novel opens almost in the tone of Raja Rao invoking goddess Kenchamma in *Kanthapura*. But what is the river's role in the novel? How is it relevant to the plot? Metaphysically, like the Ganges in *The Serpent and the Rope*? No, there is no later thematic reference to it, nor a reversion to a talk of the river, except to say that the river carried away Balan's sacred thread. As in the case of the title the novel's beginning sounds a little pretentious.

The other flaw is more integral to the structure of the plot : it is the first newspaper report about the 'Brahmin scavenger', with Ganesh's letter appended. Evidently, only someone who had knowledge about Balan's conversion could have come out with such a write up : notice this closely :

> "... We have not come across an instance of a well educated Brahmin youth who has chosen to become a scavenger anonymously. We can vouch for the truth... at the appropriate time, we hope to publish the details of this unusual human story... For the present, we are happy to publish the following letter written to the youth by his friend..." (p. 125).

But except Kuppan and his illiterate companions at Sirumudi and Pichu after he had gone to Sirumudi and Kamalapur following the lead of the newspaper story, no one could have known about this. Could Ganesh have guessed it, and guessed it so exactly? But there it is, even to the anonymous letter to the apostate. The illogic of this is so obvious that it jolts the reader. The writer used it as a deus ex-machina to move the plot to the final stage of exposure-betrayal. This may be cavilling, but we wish that he had chosen a more logical or less obvious device to accelerate the plot.

But without a doubt, the writer has started the novel with a clear, "Social purpose," though his protagonist is made to declare in the climactic phase that he had undertaken the penance for self-purification rather than for a social purpose (p. 143). The social criticism gathers momentum and culminates in Ganesh's declaration at the end that Balan's dream would be fulfilled when people start following the saints instead of merely worshiping them (p. 161). Ganesh's endeavour to spread the message of "Brotherhood of man and the Fatherhood of God" through the Bala Yogi Foundation is praiseworthy, yet one wonders if the path chosen by Balan would indeed solve the problem of social inequality and caste discrimination. Leaving aside the psycho-spiritual transformation in Balan, conversion from one caste to another would not lead to a casteless society. But rather to an inversion where the second caste would become the dominant one. As Kuppan of Sirumudi pointed out even the sub-sects among the untouchables, the chakkiliayam Paraiyans, the Malas, would not mix, intermarry or sit to meals together; and strict priority had to be observed at the funeral feeding when the gounder died. There is no basic difference between Kuppan's and Pichu's ways of thinking and that of Seshadri Iyer and Kandaswamy. Evidently, the canker is quite ubiquitious. Mere social awareness does not seem to be enough, as the 'post-exposure letters to Balan' clearly indicate only through a complete change of heart in the society can the writer's dream be realised.

But then to the extent that the protagonist is not only merely cognizant of the dead wood of tradition and orthodoxy, seeking purification in a union with an untouchable Chandri (like Pranesacharya does), but rather through a process of identification *becomes* an untouchable (and not merely an untouchable's husband), this novel is in advance of *Samskara* : and if we can set aside the few flaws in the plot we have considered above, we still have a strongly focussed tale of progress from guilt to atonement, from anguish to realisation and from solitude to love and union. This is, indeed, a thought provoking, if also a disturbing novel.

